Leadership Lessons
Learned IMPOSSIBLE
by the
DREAMER

Leadership Lessons
Learned by the IMPOSSIBLE
DREAMER

LuAn
Mitchell-Halter

**Executive
Books**

Advance Praise

LuAn Mitchell-Halter's story is riveting. I have known LuAn for a long time and journeyed with her through many of the dramatic personal, family, and corporate challenges she has survived. I have watched with admiration as she persevered, always found the seed for good and never lost faith, no matter how devastating the tragedy. This book is the true story of a remarkable woman, a remarkable life and incredible—and repeated—triumph. You will be inspired.

— Dr. Robert Schuller
The Hour of Power
CRYSTAL CATHEDRAL MINISTRIES

LuAn could be the poster child for resilience. She shares her life story as another way of reaching and helping those whose struggles sometimes obscure their belief that they can remain true to themselves and triumph over adversity. I appreciate her practical recipes for turning adversity and challenge into opportunity. Her sense of humor and her ability to maintain perspective when faced with potential trauma are a reminder to believe in love and in a spiritual connection as an ever-present source of strength.

— Claude M. Chemtob, Ph.D.
CLINICAL PROFESSOR OF PSYCHIATRY AND PEDIATRICS

The balancing act for most women is kids, husband, and a job. It usually doesn't include a dying husband in constant need of sophisticated medical care (read: transplants), a family battle over corporate holdings necessitating a lifestyle shift (i.e., moving children, husband, and pets into the family van) and then becoming Chairperson of the Board of a food company that was built from a meatpacking business, fighting off banks, bankruptcy, vultures, and predators while still raising a young family. Throw in having a high school education, being a former beauty queen, and you have amazing fiction—except for one thing. It's not fiction! This is the story of a real woman, an award-winning Canadian entrepreneur and now philanthropist, LuAn Mitchell-Halter. If you want to see how and what life lessons took Ms. Mitchell-Halter to the top despite horrendous odds, this book is a journey you must take. It is a life lesson for us all.

— Peter Dekom
ENTERTAINMENT ATTORNEY AND CO-AUTHOR, *Not on My Watch*

It is a daunting task, albeit such a pleasant one, and an extreme honour, to have been asked to offer a few words about the extraordinary author of the book you are about to read.

Actually, this is so much more than a book. It is an "E-Ticket"—for a ride ~ a journey along life's highway ~ with all its peaks and valleys, narrated by someone who, if you are fortunate enough to meet in person, let alone in the pages that follow, will send you soaring, just by her very presence.

Consider that you have been given a timeless gift, to be forever cherished, by virtue of the fact that you are able to share the most intimate feelings of, and sagely (beyond her years) wisdom of one of the Leading Women of the World.

Fasten your seatbelts! Grab a hanky ~ and put a little extra moisturizer on those laugh lines. LuAn Mitchell-Halter ~ You Rock!

— Bob Koff
CHAIRMAN, PRIVATE RESOURCE GROUP

LuAn is an inspiring speaker and author who motivates her audiences to face challenges head on, encouraging them to follow gut instinct in order to achieve success, fulfillment and happiness. With a gift for balancing family and the family business, LuAn has garnered worldwide recognition for her success in overcoming personal and financial obstacles.

— Canadian Association of Insurance and Financial Advisors

LuAn Mitchell-Halter shares her journey from being called "Elly Mae" to being named Canada's Number One Female Entrepreneur for three successive years. She uses positive thinking as well as setting a plan, listening to her instincts, and looking for the good in each situation. She has overcome obstacles that would have set anyone back, and has given so much to her family, community, and to the world. I am proud to know her. This book is an inspiration for all."

— Beverly Whipple, Ph.D., R.N., F.A.A.N.
AUTHOR AND PROFESSOR EMERITA, RUTGERS, THE STATE UNIVERSITY OF NEW JERSEY

Dear LuAn,

After reading your book yesterday evening, I was very happy. The feeling lingered into this morning. You have done a great job, and you should be very pleased. The structure of the book is excellent, with the plan to get closer to the dream, the instincts, and the seed for good. Your book is a very powerful force for good.

There are at least two important behaviors you share with the reader that I have practiced for years. First, my family like yours knows that I need my baths to think and meditate. It is a very powerful tool. I try to do it every day, and I feel bad when I do not. I actually prefer to shower than to wash, but I cannot think in a shower.

Then I also make my own movies in my head to look at the future. I can fill them in and change the scenario to fit different possibilities and outcome.

Many other details struck home. Your book is very personal, and also universal. I believe the forgiving paragraphs at the end are very important. You share your intense physical reaction to negative energy, and your need to keep the power to remain peaceful.

Finally, on the business side, I can say you have a clear impact. I am in the middle of an increase in capital in my company that manages all the big chefs contracts I have, for instance international rights for El Bulli, the number one restaurant in the world, and several others, including Lea Linster, the only woman ever to win the Bocuse d'Or, who has two restaurants in Luxembourg, and should be included in the Leading Women of the World.

My company now has a capital of 3,250,000 Euros, of which I control 95 percent. I am raising outside my family over a million, mostly in Switzerland, while keeping control. Well, I have felt bad for six weeks about some potential investors. Thanks to your book, I have decided to follow my instincts, and change those investors. As a result, this morning I finally felt so good about it. Thank you! It is the kind of problem that is very difficult to share, but your book did it, it helped me resolve the issue.

As you say, all families have problems, but they do not all make headlines.

In our case, in 1989 we had the front page of the weekend edition of the Financial Times with the title, "Better than Dallas," describing our fights with our cousins, and the 70 lawsuits. We sold our shares in Remy Martin and Cointreau a year later. Fortunately, at my generation, it is mostly forgiven. For my parents, it is very much alive, and I am going to send them two or three pages from your book! It might help.

Thank you again. Your book had a major impact, both in an emotional way, making me very happy, and leading to a very practical decision to change my business life.

— Edouard Cointreau

FOUNDER AND PRESIDENT OF GOURMAND BOOKS,
AND THE GOURMAND WORLD COOKBOOK AWARDS

Leadership Lessons Learned
By The Impossible Dreamer

Published by
Executive Books
206 West Allen Street
Mechanicsburg, PA 17055

CIP data available from the Library of Congress

ISBN-13: 978-1-933715-06-3
ISBN-10: 1-933715-06-5

PRINTED IN THE UNITED STATES OF AMERICA

Dedication

*To my dear friend,
Anita Alberts*

She made her transition in style from this world to the next, leaving us with a legacy of love. Founder and former president of the Los Angeles based *Star Group,* she worked tirelessly to recognize many unsung heroes of the world. Her foresight and dedication established the *Leading Women Entrepreneurs of the World* celebrations in which I had the great honor of being inducted into in Madrid, Spain, 2001.

Contents

FOREWORD — xiii

ACKNOWLEDGMENTS — xv

INTRODUCTION — xix

CHAPTER 1: Listen to Your Instincts — 1

CHAPTER 2: Surround Yourself with People Who Inspire You — 9

CHAPTER 3: Act from a Position of Hope, Not Fear — 21

CHAPTER 4: Don't Give in to Long Odds — 33

CHAPTER 5: Define Your Dream — 45

CHAPTER 6: Seek Alliances to Support Your Dream — 59

CHAPTER 7: Never Give Up on Your Dream — 69

CHAPTER 8: No Dream Is Achieved Alone — 93

CHAPTER 9: Let Your Priorities Lead You — 117

CHAPTER 10: Protect Your Power — 145

CHAPTER 11: Giving Back Offers Tremendous Rewards — 155

READING GROUP GUIDE — 169

ABOUT LUAN — 175

Foreword

*History has demonstrated
that the most notable winners usually encountered
heartbreaking obstacles before they triumphed.
They won because they refused to become
discouraged by their defeats.*

B. C. Forbes said those words in 1917, shortly before founding Forbes magazine. Eighty-five years later his axiom rings especially true, as LuAn Mitchell-Halter would appreciate. She has been through a passel of troubles and has persevered, enjoying abundant success as measured by the essentials that most of us pursue: unyielding love, ample security, and sweet comfort.

At first glance, LuAn's life story reads like an overwrought script for a bad made-for-cable movie. It involves tragedy and triumph, corporate intrigue and family feuds, litigation and compromise, and love and hate—and the occasional death threat. Were she hawking this in a Hollywood pitch meeting—and if she hasn't yet, we can be sure she will soon after this book comes out—LuAn could offer a de rigueur summary: This is *Working Girl* meets *Love Story*.

Whew! It is all a bit much, and certainly it is a good copy.

Yet, in *Paper Doll*, LuAn spends little time dwelling solipsistically on these fevered events. Instead, she focuses on learning and leveraging life's lessons to turn adversity into opportunity. It is what real leaders in business manage to do all the time. She seems most concerned with preaching these lessons to those who will listen: how to trust your instincts, build an inner circle of support, set new priorities and define your dreams so you can chase after the biggest ones.

The cynics among you might point out an undeniable truth: Sure, it's easy for her to say she got lucky and made herself a millionaire. And, admittedly, sometimes with advice like this, it is hard to know which points are profound and which ones offer a blinding glimpse of the obvious. What's important is that LuAn Mitchell-Halter feels these things deeply, believes in them wholeheartedly, and now endeavors to share them with you.

— Dennis Kneale
MANAGING EDITOR FOR *Forbes* MAGAZINE

Acknowledgments

"Spiritual Thanks" to the angels that surround me . . .
Who give me insights, and kept me safe
Eternal Beings that I have with me always . . .

My beloved late husband: Fred Mitchell

My Earth Family:

My dear, dear husband Reese—Who has stood tall by me through it all, loves and accepts our children as their father, and strengthens my convictions—all the while still shining a bright, indelible spirit and loving me in ways I could only have dreamed before he came into my life to make it real.

My children . . . Freddie, Ryan, and Jinjara—Who have been my greatest teachers, and always seen me as whole and complete . . . even when the rest of the world would have thrown me out with the bathwater. They sacrificed, and persevered with Mommy on so many roads. I am a blessed and chosen woman to be their Mom.

My mother and father: Anna and Peter Gingara—Who taught me love, and old-fashioned values that prevail.

I have felt wrapped in the wings of *The Eternal* Nola Halter—Mother of my dear husband Reese. Her love and guiding light helped to create the man I love. I shall thank her forever.

My beautiful sisters—Emily and Debbie. Each a symphony bringing music to my life—*and* to my strong and precious brother Rick. You have believed in me, and were always there with me on this journey with all its ups and downs. We have watched families torn apart, and you have always accepted my choices, and embraced my partners and children.

And especially my *Sis,* Judy, we are the lucky ones to get to work together. Without you I would never have dared to believe. You saw in me the things I could not see . . . you have given of yourself day and night to see this book reach fruition, and have always been my friend. (Although you did get Dad's nose—I wanted that!) YOU always get the good stuff.

Thank you all for your love.

My Soul Sisters:

Marie Sembalerus-Lee—Who became my friend when no one else wanted to. My high school friend who never left. We screwed up a few times together, Marie, but we never gave up on an opportunity to set the record straight.

Debbie Luican—Who believed in my story and helped to take it to the world! You are beautiful, and brilliant. How blessed am I to be with you on this journey.

Julie Chrystyn—My brilliant shining star . . . who has a gift to look beyond what others see and express, so we can all understand. You bring laughter to the world with your gentle words . . . healing me many times just when I needed it.

Anna Ouroumian—The Warrior! You are Amazing! A force for good, a Tsunami!

Bev Dubois—She never stops . . . my marathon girl! Long, long talks . . . we have the gift. The meeting can wait!

Carol Suchan—Whose turbulent life is a testimony for all the world! Never give up . . . you are a great friend . . . a real friend . . . judged by many . . . but never judging others. Bigger than life!

Angela Mospanchuk—Angie, you are more my sister than my niece. Those times alone, having kids together, playing as little girls, sharing apartments—you have always made yourself available for me . . . never judged me . . . always hugged me. Now we have a new generation to nurture together.

Christy Johnson—Who has never said a bad word about anyone since I have known her! We met in kindergarten . . . as Moms how blessed we are . . . all those Palm Springs events! Tumbleweed snowmen! Wow!

Patti Gribow—Who said, "Girl, you're as great as the best of them! You go, girl! Speak it out!" Thanks, Patti . . . Thanks for being on the team.

Margaret Jurca—Who overcame—physically . . . mentally . . . and spiritually. A builder of the highest order!

Barb Stone-Bakstad—Who refused to listen to gossip and tripe . . . a woman who isn't afraid to speak out . . . who taught me love after loss . . . never judging by appearances.

Cheryl Womack—An incredible lady . . . beautiful gracious dear Cheryl. You are continuing the mission. I am so proud you included me without even knowing me. You believed . . . you shared . . . you taught me—you invited me in. You took a chance on me . . . I will never forget your kindness.

Bobbie Dunphy—You called when others forgot; you helped me be strong when I thought I'd faint . . . *And* Michael Dunphy—you knew the energy of the land. The times you carried Fred when he was too weak to move. You loved the people like we did—you saved lives. You both let me cry . . . you wiped my tears . . . Bobbie and Michael, you are a couple who inspire all couples.

To the Women Leaders of the World:

To *all* the beautiful leading Women Entrepreneurs of the World!—wherever and whomever you are—and my Women's Leadership Board at Harvard University's John F. Kennedy School of Government. Your way is better than any "beauty pagent!" *Your* beauty defies!

To My Pillars:

Dr. Robert Schuller, a longtime friend and magnificent spiritual anchor, and his wife Arvella, my *other* MOM. I salute you. I love you!

Dr. Tom Costa—My spiritual teacher, mentor, counselor, and practitioner. You have helped me remain footed on solid ground during some difficult times when I began to get "sucked" into the winds of life! You let me know I could call at any hour, and never left me alone.

Wayne Cline—My dear friend. I know how you loved Anita, and your mission together, in many ways, sparked mine. Thank you for your undying efforts and belief in us all. Losing someone you love is tough . . . you remain honorable. Therefore, *she* lives on.

A special heartfelt thanks for support in this book, and in so many other ways to Bill Peterson, and Catherine Bell.

And last, but not least, Herman Wilkinson—As a long-time dedicated Mitchell's employee, you are a true hero to the working class. You went out on a limb to take the truth to the masses as an insider who *walked the talk*. You risked it all. You are truly a good man, and have been like a brother to me—and Fred.

Bless you all . . . I am a better person because of knowing *each* of you. You have touched the lives of *all* whose path you have encountered—even if just for a moment.

I shall seize these moments forever and plant seeds from my experiences . . . you are eternally a part of the chemistry of my core.

— *LuAn*

Introduction

E X T R A !

LuAn Mitchell made millions doing what?

Maybe some people grow up with a sense they will live their life in the headlines or be a star. It's certainly nothing that I foresaw or sought. And if someone told me 20 years ago that my children would still be reading headlines about me today, I never would have believed it. But the reality is that for much of my adult life, I have lived in the spotlight for one reason or another. And an important lesson I have learned along the way is that at any moment, we can take charge and write our *own* headlines—and the storylines that go under them.

It can be very difficult to be publicly criticized or to read things about yourself or others you care about that you know aren't true. It's so frustrating to think that people are reading—and believing—things that are just plain wrong. And even when the attention is positive, there are the challenges of managing expectations and demands on your time. But I won't complain. I lead a full, rewarding life. I enjoy every second of it. I've found another seed for good in being in the public eye: I can help people. Today, that is both my mission *and* my passion—giving back. I do that by being totally honest and open about my life, and what I have learned.

If you are so down and out that you think you'll never find the strength to get up again, or if someone or something kicked you where it hurts and you're down for the count, don't get nasty. Get wise to the winner's circle—enter it and never leave.

If you are fighting for something you believe in despite long odds and in the face of great opposition, or you're being told it can't be done—you're nuts, I've been there, too. If your world has been turned upside down and you just don't know if you can cope, if every medical journal says it's over, I've been there, too.

All you have to do is get up, stand straight and tall. Get up! Put pride in your stride and do what it takes to move closer to your dream. Listen to your instincts. They are there for you to draw on. Remain vigilant for the seed of good that emerges from every experience no matter what it looks like on the outside. And above all, have faith— faith in your dream, faith in your instincts, and faith in yourself.

SMALL TOWN BEAUTY QUEEN LUAN MITCHELL MAY HAVE MARRIED SASKATCHEWAN'S LEADING SCION, BUT THAT DIDN'T LAND HER ON EASY STREET

Always looking for opportunities to meet people and see more of the world, I began modeling at the age of 20. I entered a local beauty pageant . . . and won! In 1984, I advanced to the Miss Canada pageant. This was an exhilarating time with lots of exciting opportunities presenting themselves. But when I met the man who would change my life, I didn't even realize it—I was too caught up in the whirlwind called my life. Fortunately, Fred Mitchell was persistent.

And when I finally took notice, I fell madly in love.

Fred Mitchell was 14 years my senior, and the president of one of the largest companies in Western Canada, Intercontinental Packers. When he proposed, I thought all my dreams were coming true. But shortly before our wedding, Fred received a grim medical diagnosis: He was suffering from cystic fibrosis. It had gone undetected for years. Not only would this threaten his life, the doctors said, but also it was highly unlikely Fred could father children, something we both wanted. Fred and I took this news in our stride—we had a happy wedding and were later delighted to discover that, against all odds, I was pregnant. Freddie, Jr. was born in 1988, a healthy bouncing nine-pound bundle of joy. And we would go on to have two more "miracles" come into our family.

Fred's health problems worsened rapidly. We couldn't have imagined that his health could deteriorate so dramatically. At one point, this man who stood almost six feet tall weighed only 115 pounds, just five pounds more than his petite 5 foot 4 inch wife. Our only hope was an experimental and highly risky heart/double lung transplant. Fred was near death when he received a life-saving transplant in 1990. His recovery was bumpy, long, and slow. But eventually, he was able to devote his time and energy to his family's business again.

Soon, he was embroiled in a nasty and very public legal dispute with his family. We risked almost everything as we fought for the company and its people. At one point, we were living in a dilapidated Chevy van with our three preschool children; two Rottweilers; and our toy poodle, Babykins. But our deep commitment to each other and the dream, coupled with perseverance, paid off: We eventually gained control of the pork processing business we had fought so hard for.

Just as we reached our settlement, we were hit with another cosmic two-by-four: The company was in soft receivership, and the bank was insisting that they be repaid all of their loans in full. We raised over $30 million in a matter of only months and got down to the serious business of turning around the company's fortunes. We renamed the company "Mitchell's Gourmet Foods," expanded the plant's capacity, and grew our range of products. Employment was now increasing under our leadership and sales were healthy. Fred and I were getting ready to take the company public. Fred was recognized with a Turnaround Entrepreneur of the Year award in 1998. Then out of the blue, tragedy struck. During a visit to the Stanford Medical Center, Fred suddenly died.

Instead of Cashing in, His Widow Boldly Takes Over the Boardroom

That was undoubtedly my lowest moment. I had lost my husband and my three children had lost their devoted father. And before we had even said our prayers and buried Fred, the bloodthirsty vultures started to circle. The eager buyers for Mitchell's were lining up— and they weren't doing it quietly. They assumed that I, the little widow lady, was an easy mark—that I would give up on the business and its people after Fred died. They assumed that rather than risk my equity in a company that had just lost its guiding light, I'd take the safe route and cash out. They assumed I'd retire a multi-millionaire. But the vultures assumed wrong.

If I had left Mitchell's, there was a real danger a new owner would simply scoop our company's hard-earned market share and close us down. The livelihoods of more than 1,000 families would vaporize. The spin off effects would be devastating for the area's hog producers like my late grandfather. To everyone's surprise, this piece of fluff stepped into an active role with Mitchell's as chair of the Board. I oversaw a strategic alliance that enabled us to expand the company vastly. We opened a new state-of-the-art facility and grew to become one of the leading suppliers of meat products and processed foods in North America. And I was delighted to be recognized as Canada's #1 Female Entrepreneur three years running. Being acknowledged for my mind has always been more of an honor (and much more to my liking) than any beauty pageant could have ever provided.

My Three Easy Steps

I can't count how many times people ask how I've been able to continually overcome adversity. I was called a "survivor" long before the hit TV show was even invented. But in fact, my winning formula is very simple. Whatever the situation (and you must stay focused on the situation, not the players)—whether I'm dealing with the death of someone I love, considering a strategic alliance or public offering for my company, making an important decision about my family or my lifestyle, or about pouring my heart out in this book—I always follow my three easy steps:

- Make a realistic plan that will get you closer to your dream,
- Follow your God-given instincts,
- Find the seed for good.

Throughout this book, you'll see how these strategies have never failed me. In the good times and the bad, I keep following these three steps religiously. This is my game plan for overcoming obstacles, doing good in this world, and leading a happy, fulfilling life. And I know these steps can work for you, too. Let me take you there by the hand—and remember that I've been there, too.

Some people may look at me and think, "It was easy for her—she married the successful CEO of a large company." But that's the fairy tale, not the real story. These people didn't see me having my heart torn out repeatedly looking after a chronically ill spouse. They didn't see me striding the halls of the Stanford Medical Center, my baby in a backpack, pacing as my husband rebounded from a risky and miraculous transplant. They didn't see us in Cardio Rehab or fighting rejection. They didn't see me when I was about to hock my precious wedding ring when we were fighting to save the company and its special people. And they didn't see me put my fist through a bathroom wall after my husband drew his last breath. No, it hasn't been easy, and it hasn't been simple for me. But believe me, if I can do it, you can, too.

I have been fortunate in my life to be able to cut through the public's image of me as just a "paper doll," a piece of fluff—a headliner (someone who was *only* defined by the clothes she wore). Or thought to look good in a bikini and get to the core of my being where the seeds are contained—seeds for good. A person who is multi-dimensional, a builder. A person who chooses what she decides to *wear* with no cover-up! A person who is fully exposed on life's journey based in the undying wisdom of life eternal and believing in miracles.

New Chapter for Mitchell

My personal life has also taken more surprising turns. When I least expected it, I fell in love with another extraordinary man. Dr. Reese Halter and I married in 2002, and he has become a loving father to our three children. My involvement with Mitchell's has wound down recently. Recognizing that the company needed to continue to grow and seize opportunities and to do this needed shareholders prepared to act who had much deeper pockets than mine, I sold my shares in the company.

I've learned a lot along the way. People constantly say they can't believe what I've gone through, that all of this could happen to one person with the few spins around the sun I have journeyed. It gives me a tremendous sense of satisfaction to know that people can gain something from the lessons I've learned—and that they can do it without the hard knocks I've endured!

I've painstakingly struggled to write this book. But as I write, it is always in keeping with my three steps. This is the story of my life based on *my perspective* as the one living it. It is written with love for the people who come up to me after I've spoken at one of my many public speaking engagements, luncheons, and seminars. It's for the people who are very interested and moved by what I have to say as I share the lessons I've learned. They tell me that I inspired them and ask, "Where's your book?" I've written it for courageous entrepreneurs who have an idea and might just need a gentle push. I've written it for our Mitchell's employees whose love and support sustained me in my most difficult hours. And I've written it for anyone who has a dream and recognizes how exhilarating it would be to achieve that dream.

In my life, I've come to a place of realizing that the true art of being completely centered and focused, amidst the fast and turbulent journey in this sometimes wild and crazy world we live in, comes *not* from transporting ourselves next to a babbling brook—but it comes, in fact, from learning to reach and maintain a calm and balanced center next to a babbling *person*.

You are worth putting it all "on the line." Don't let anyone or anything stop you. Don't just dream your dreams and tuck them away out of sight—get up and make them come true. They are yours! Take hold of them now! Let's plant seeds together and make a garden. You have always had the claim ticket.

Please read on. I can teach you what I learned. Go get 'em, Tiger!

Chapter One

LIFE LESSON:

Listen to Your Instincts

Each of us has a little voice inside us that can help us when making difficult decisions. Sometimes it's easy to recognize this voice—you can feel it deep in your gut. I believe our God-given instincts tap into our deeper knowledge. They help us uncover what we already know. Our instincts are an unconscious skill, a survival mechanism that can be used repeatedly to great advantage. Whether you think of it as following your instincts or going with your gut, I know you can't go wrong if you are true to that voice deep within you.

*LuAn's story contains
just as much tragedy as triumph.*

— *Airlines* **magazine, November 2001**

"**Y**ou've ruined your life," my mother said coldly when I was 16 years old. At that time, stunned and at the lowest moment in my short life, I thought she was right. I had done the worst thing a teenage girl in a small town could do: I was pregnant and starting to show. This was my first encounter with adversity—I had no idea how much more there was to come! In some ways, I've been trying to prove my mother wrong and regain my sense of worth ever since. One thing I knew for sure is I would never say things like that to my kids—it really hurt. Her voice rang in my ears and heart for years.

Life was pretty simple for me as a child. My doting dad was a math teacher at our local school and my mom was a stellar homemaker and great cook who taught 4H to the kids in our community. Over the years, we lived in a few small farming towns in Western Canada. My four siblings—three sisters and one brother—were older than me with a bit of an age gap, so in some ways I felt like I was an only child. I had just turned 14 when we moved to the big city of Saskatoon; at least that's how I felt about this city of about 200,000 people.

Suddenly, I went from being the popular girl to being the victim of ridicule and completely friendless at school. My parents had placed me in a Catholic high school to "keep me pure." I liked to wear fuzzy cotton plaid shirts and overalls, which was pretty standard in Hicksville. But for a girl in the city, this would never do. One day a teacher called me "Elly Mae," after the bumpkin girl on the *Beverly Hillbillies*, in front of the whole Christian Ethics class, and the nickname stuck. From that day on, when I walked down the hall at school, some of the kids would salute and call me "Elly Mae"—a slam against my rural roots and my looks.

One winter day, a couple of girls from the school who felt sorry for me and were desperate to help me fit in showed up at my house after school and asked my mom for some money so they could help me buy new clothes. "Someone's going to kill her if she doesn't fix this up," they pleaded. "What's wrong with her clothes?" was Mom's stony reply, and any hopes of a shopping expedition were dashed. I hid in my room, scared out of my wits—I had already been threatened by a girl from a gang (something new to me) at school earlier that day.

You Know How Life Sometimes Throws Speed Bumps in Your Way? LuAn Mitchell Got the Everest Variety

I was entering my final year of high school when I discovered I was pregnant (which sent the nuns and my parents reeling). I met my first real "he's the one" boyfriend when I was 15. I was far from active socially but did give in to sharing a few beers with him one night. Big mistake. "The other girls will" was all I could remember and a lot of pain for a long time after. A few months later, my mother and I went to the doctor together. When I timidly asked for a prescription for the Pill in my private session, the doctor insisted on doing a pregnancy test first. Oops. I was pregnant. My mother's first words in the elevator upon hearing this news were, "You've ruined your life now." My father was equally angry and disapproving, and before long, my boyfriend was out of the picture. You can imagine the reaction of the nuns who taught at my high school. I was scared and devastated.

There was some pressure on me to forget the whole thing and just get an abortion, but I wouldn't even consider that option. *After all it wasn't the baby's fault; why should it suffer because I made a mistake,* I thought. My plan was to have the baby and give it up for adoption. At first I continued to live in a small room in my parents' home, but it was agonizing. The shame they felt—which I also felt—the way they looked at me, the tears—were making us all miserable. Once, when my parents were having friends over for dinner, my mom told me: "LuAn, stay in your room while our guests are here. Don't ask questions—just do it."

I knew she was ashamed, and she didn't want to have to explain my condition. I will never forget how utterly rejected and humiliated I felt as I spent that evening alone in my room with my fat, achy body. My ankles were swollen and my breasts were huge. My butt was gargantuan. I hated myself and felt that my life was over. This self-loathing had a deep and profound effect on me. Soon, I ran away from home to live with my sister's family on a military base in northern Alberta. After being kicked off the base, I lived with my brother and his girlfriend in an apartment in downtown Saskatoon. I continued to correspond with my high school studies, mailing my work back to my teachers.

Despite the emotional turmoil, it was physically an easy pregnancy. My beautiful daughter was born in June 1978. While all my friends were graduating from high school in pretty prom dresses and tuxes, I was learning how to nurse a baby and change diapers. I named her "Jacqueline" after the actress Jacqueline Bissett, whom I admired. After seeing my precious baby, I started to have doubts about giving her up for adoption. In a total turnaround, my family was now pressuring me to keep her, and I gave in happily—she was part of me, and I would do right by her.

My parents welcomed us into their home, but they couldn't afford to support us. I was too young to qualify for welfare, so I started working three jobs—as a cosmetics clerk in a department store, in the kitchen at a fish and chips joint, and taking in other children for babysitting at night. Every night I would literally fall into bed, exhausted beyond belief. Then the baby would start crying. I'd stumble out of bed, pick her up and pretty soon, I would start crying. There I was, a child with a child, barely coping. It seemed that both of us were crying all the time, resenting each other, strangers yet blood relatives. What was happening? What kind of a crazy world was this?

The city of Saskatoon has a big river running through it, so it's often called the "City of Bridges." When things were particularly bleak for me, I considered committing suicide more than once. I thought about which of the bridges I would jump from. What I couldn't figure out in my fragile state was what to do with the baby. Would I take her with me? Leave her for my mom and dad to care for? Who would take her? I can see now that I was severely depressed. Fortunately, the thoughts of suicide didn't last for long.

TAKE MY BABY—PLEASE

One night, I fell into a deep sleep while feeding Jacqueline on my twin bed. The two of us fell out of bed, toppling onto the floor together. She wasn't hurt, but I was terrified at what could have happened. What if I wouldn't have woken up? What if she couldn't breathe? I realized that my first instinct was right: This baby deserved to have parents who could take care of her properly. I was messed up. My parents were older now, and my father was stricken with Alzheimer's disease. There was only so much they could do to help me; I had to grow up fast!

The next day, I dialed Social Services and agreed to put the baby up for adoption. They picked her up that afternoon. My parents sat stunned, grief-stricken beyond words. I will never forget the raw deep-seated torment I felt as I sat on my parent's front porch, watching through tears as the woman's car drove away with my baby in it. Tucked into her car seat was a tearstained letter written to my daughter on my Holly Hobby stationery, a young mother's plea for forgiveness. My legs felt like lead and so did my heart. I didn't know if I would ever find the strength to stand up and continue with life. I hated myself, this world, and God himself. But I did get up.

As an adult, I know that I share that experience with many. And when I did, I was a different person. I promised myself that I would always be able to support my family and myself. I would forgive her birth dad for hurting us so. Most importantly, I would never be in that situation again. No one was going to make me stay in this place for the rest of my life. I refused!

Right then, I vowed to listen to my instincts, not the opinions of other people. Then I hugged my parents, packed my bags, and walked out the door. I was on my own.

MY PLAN TO GET ME CLOSER TO MY DREAM:

Work three jobs, do whatever it takes to support my baby and myself.

MY INSTINCTS:

Listen to the voice within, not the opinions of other people.

THE SEED FOR GOOD:

I gained a lifelong determination to always be able to support my family and myself.

Chapter Two

LIFE LESSON:

Surround Yourself with People Who Inspire You

I recognized at an early age that we become like those who surround us. Throughout my life, I've made an effort to surround myself with people who inspire me. You can, too.

Look for people whom you admire at your workplace, in your line of work, or in your community. Read about people who achieve success, overcome adversity, seek adventure— whatever turns you on! No matter what situation you're in, you can, in some way, surround yourself with the kind of people you would like to become. Learn from them and draw energy from their story. Then use that knowledge and power to propel yourself closer to your own dream.

She's a Big Hit

Miss Saskatoon, 22-year-old LuAn Gingara splashes fellow contests in the Miss Canada pageant at the girls' hotel in Toronto. Thirty-eight young women are vying for the national title.

— Toronto Star, 1984

*G*irls from the wrong side of the tracks aren't supposed to enter beauty pageants, much less win and go on to the national competition. But fortunately, I've never paid much attention to what I was or wasn't supposed to do according to the world at large and the opinions of others. I got launched on the road to Miss Canada by my sister Judy.

At the time, I was taking courses in hair styling and aesthetics and night courses in literature. My goal was to work on cruise ships and see the world—maybe work for a magazine on the side writing articles. I was very focused on learning skills that I could always use to support myself and give me a safety net. I learned about the importance of being self-sufficient the hard way, a hard lesson I was not going to repeat in this lifetime if I could help it.

Miss Saskatoon 1984

I've always had a love of learning instilled in me by my father. After finally completing high school, I enrolled at a local beauty college. I also took courses in creative writing and broadcasting. But for a girl in my position, from the "wrong" side of town, living in a little apartment, surrounded with drunks and loud mouths, with no money but lots of ambition, there weren't many options.

One opportunity I did spot was beauty pageants. My new figure wasn't too bad considering I was 36-24-34. Some things had resettled nicely after my pregnancy. I figured beauty pageants were a way to be recognized, have a voice, and see the world beyond the city limits. When I see the young people on TV shows like *American Idol* today, I see the same hopes and dreams that I had in my early 20s. They're looking for their big break, some way of getting ahead, and being someone—mattering in the world, just as I was.

My faithful sister Judy knew that I was interested in entering the regional beauty pageant and just needed a little push. She helped me get the headshot photos I needed to apply for the competition. I was a bit hesitant—there were still those voices in my head, the kids at high school who called me "Elly Mae," and my inner demons who called me a sinner.

Fortunately, Judy gave me the encouragement and support I needed. I entered the regional competition, along with nearly 1,000 other entrants. It goes was something like this: They narrow the competition down to 200, then 10, then one. The day I got the call that I won and was off to the national competition, I almost fainted. I remember thinking to myself at the time: *I knew I could do it!* The year I spent as a regional representative was an extraordinary experience full of learning and training that would help me later in life. Throughout my life, there have been people who were only too quick to say something couldn't be done, and I've been only too happy to prove them wrong.

When I won the regional pageant, one of the letters I received from a high school friend read, "You know, when you first moved to this city, you were the ugliest, scraggliest farm girl we ever saw. And what happened? Look at you now—you're Miss Saskatoon!" A few months later, I was flying across the country to the national competition, my banner proudly displayed across my silk blouse. I felt reborn!

THE ADVANCEMENT OF WOMEN IN SOCIETY

Prior to the Miss Canada pageant, I started thinking seriously about what I would do for the "talent" segment of the competition. At that time, it was common for contestants to sing, play the piano, or dance. But I wasn't particularly talented at any of those. I believed that one of my talents was speaking. I was hosting a talk show back home and a radio call-in show, too, so I decided to do a speech and chose as my subject successful women in society. I spent weeks at the university library, researching women like Margaret Thatcher, Geraldine Ferraro, and Eleanor Roosevelt. I even put together a slide show to support my speech. I titled it "The Advancement of Women in Society." I dressed in a business suit, wore pumps, and pinned my hair back into a tight French roll.

As you can imagine, my presentation went over like a lead balloon. The matronly look flopped, and so did I! Keep in mind, at this pageant, like many others, a big part of the program is the hot-bod in the swimsuit competition. I discovered that the long never-ending runways are positioned so that when the girls come out in their swimsuits, the judges seated below have a bird's eye view up at their crotches. Think of my speech about intelligent and capable women leaders in this environment. I can see now how naïve I was!

I didn't win—far from it—but the Miss Canada pageant was a fabulous experience. I met some lovely ladies, and I learned so much. I've always believed that you should surround yourself with the people you want to emulate—be with those whom you want to become. And in fact, this national pageant gave me the opportunity to do this. While I physically fit the bill in the world's eye as a beauty pageant contestant, I was really a misfit of the highest order in the pageant world. But my tireless research for my speech introduced me to some fascinating, powerful women, albeit in the library or my mind. The women who really inspired me were the people I included in my speech. I longed to be like them. I pinned quotations from them on the wall of my bedroom and had stacks of books about these women all over my apartment. I learned about the importance of being strong, having a vision, and being willing to break down barriers. Most importantly, I realized the importance of pursuing your passions in life. "Bet you could get in *Playboy*," my friends chided. "Not likely," I retorted. Why couldn't anyone see the *real* me! How would I survive?

I also learned about the importance of tuning out the naysayers. If I let critical people stop me from pursuing my dreams, I would have achieved very little in this life. My beauty pageant experience was the first time that I simply didn't listen to the people who said I had no chance, so why was I even trying? It's so easy to stand back and criticize, never taking chances. But where will that get you? I saw an opportunity, and I went after it. And more often than not, I succeeded—just being there opened some doors for me repeatedly. I interviewed with a national TV network while at the pageant and even received a job offer for some on-air work with them, something I had long aspired to. But while I was considering that opportunity and a move to the really big city after my term expired, a chance encounter changed my life.

Happy Friday—Fred

Shortly after the Miss Canada pageant, I was working during the day at a beauty salon and evenings as a hostess in a nightclub, filming my television show in between. Having just split with my insulting ("Oh, you think you're really something now") boyfriend, I needed the extra job to make the rent. The last thing I was looking for was a new boyfriend or getting tied down. It was a quiet evening, and I was sitting at the front check-in reading a motivational book, *I Ain't Well but I Sure Am Better*. Fred and his buddy Herb wandered in for a drink, and I seated them. According to Herb, Fred was instantly taken with me. Before they left, Fred asked me out. I was quite short with him, responding that I didn't date customers—I didn't have a high opinion of the club or its patrons. I was just making ends meet by being there. "But I've never been here before in my life!" Fred protested. "My friend just brought me here for a quick drink after work."

It didn't take Fred long to find out how to reach me. He had watched my television show, and I was Miss Saskatoon after all! A few days later, a fresh beautiful bouquet of red roses arrived at the beauty salon where I worked. The card read simply: "Happy Friday—Fred." Later that day, Fred called my workplace and asked me out for lunch. I accepted and soon discovered what a brilliant, funny, kind man he was. We became friends. I discovered who he was—a local big wig. Fred was the president of Intercontinental Packers, one of the biggest businesses in our region. The company had several meat-packing plants in Western Canada. There I was dating this corporate heavyweight. After I said I was going to never get off track again—I was a woman entrepreneur, I was a career woman. We only had a couple of dates before Fred went on a six-week trip to California. At that point, I wasn't sure if we would ever see each other again. We were worlds apart.

LuAn's Got a Treat for You

It was my next headline that brought Fred Mitchell back into my life. I was in the beautiful city of Calgary when a photographer stopped me on the street. He worked for the local newspaper, he explained, and they were looking for a pretty girl to do a promotion. Was I interested? "Sure," I replied. And one day later, there I was on the cover of the newspaper wearing a Calgary Sun T-shirt. It was a promotion for an NHL playoff game. The caption read, "LuAn's got a treat for you. Like our snappy Sun T-shirts? Miss Saskatoon was kind enough to model one for us yesterday. You can win two of the shirts, empty of course, by guessing the score of tomorrow night's playoff game between the Calgary Flames and the Edmonton Oilers."

This happened to be the day Fred was returning from California, and he was handed one of the newspapers on his flight home. I guess that was a sign to him that I was supposed to be in his life, because he called me as soon as he returned to Saskatoon. I was preparing to move to Toronto and had just received a movie offer even though I didn't act! "Oh, my gosh," he said. "They eat up girls like you and spit them out. My family was involved in show business. Please meet me. I want to help you. You could get hurt out there." I agreed to get together, and we started dating.

The funding for the movie fell through, but I had other plans. Fred was supportive of my entrepreneurial ventures from the first days of our relationship. Shortly after we met, I opened a spa and modeling school called "Chez L.A."—many of my friends called me "L.A." in those days for LuAn.

When I look back at this first business, I realize what a bold venture it was. There I was, 23 years old, calmly asking a bank manager for a loan, even though I had no collateral to offer and my parents couldn't co-sign for the loan. But this is where my willingness to seize opportunities came in handy.

Several months earlier, I called a popular local magazine and offered to be their beauty correspondent. I prepared and sent off sample articles. The magazine editor agreed, and I started a column under the heading of the local "Beauty Expert." I wrote about everything from hair transplants to sun tanning booths to spring fashions.

As my profile rose, more opportunities came my way. I started my modeling school, and I started a style program on our local radio station. I was hosting my television talk show and had lots of fun doing investigative interviews, reports from events, and doing hair and make-up for famous bands performing in the area. By the time I entered the bank manager's office, I was a recognizable face in the city. I think that's why he granted me the $20,000 loan that very same day.

LEARNING A LIFE LESSON

Chez L.A. was a crash course in business for me. It was a full-service salon, offering aesthetics, massage, hair styling, and a busy modeling school and agency. I learned about hiring people, keeping the books, marketing, purchasing, and so much more. But perhaps the most important thing I learned was to always trust my instincts above and beyond all else. As my business grew, I had to hire more and more staff. One of my assistant managers was a wild young woman who always gave me a funny feeling. She had the qualifications, and she did a good job. In this industry, you've got your share of characters, but I was reluctant to trust her completely.

One night, I got an alarming call from the police: Someone was breaking into Chez L.A. When I arrived at the shop, I saw the police with my assistant manager and a strange guy I had never seen before. "Oh, no. There's been a mistake," I explained, "she has a key; she works for me." But when the police pointed out that she was loading expensive computers and equipment into the back of a large truck, I realized that my own employee was trying to rip me off. My instincts had been right. I just wasn't listening. It would have been inconvenient to look for a replacement in my busiest season, so I ignored my alarms. From then on, I started listening to my gut no matter what the season. And I've become known for my finely-tuned instincts. Fred used to rely on my instincts periodically when making business or personal decisions.

My 11th Commandment

I live by an 11th Commandment: Go Gut. This means going with your gut feeling, listening to your instincts, and going for the gusto. It's an important part of getting rid of paralyzing fear and living an extraordinary life.

When I have the opportunity to speak to students, at women's groups, or in corporate gatherings, one of my main messages is to look for the answers within you. Take a fresh perspective—a new vantage point. If you're making an important decision, you don't have to call eight friends frantically for their advice. You already have the advice you need—ultimately you are the only person who knows what's right for you. Be honest with yourself, and trust your instincts. Let your friends off the hook. Don't try to reel them into your private world—they don't have the same motivation. They may even mean well but could put water instead of another log on the fire and prevent you from going ahead.

Often, there are times when our heads tell us one thing, our instincts tell us another, and our heart may tell us yet another. How do we know which voice to listen to when they don't all agree? How do you unscramble the reception—"pull in the antennae?" The trick is to zone in on one station.

Many people have buried their instincts under layers of conditioning. Some of us are held back by the conditioning we received growing up, our parents' protective voices cautioning us: "You'll never make a living doing that." A good friend of mine still regrets not following her passion for singing and acting. When she was choosing electives in high school, her parents directed her away from drama and music, telling her she needed practical skills like typing even though she was talented and passionate. She still remembers the feeling of betrayal when she realized they were telling her they didn't believe she'd succeed on stage because of *their* own fears. Just trying to "protect" their little girl! But what if they were wrong? Twenty years later, she still feels the pain.

Usually, it's fear that stops us from believing in ourselves or someone else. We worry about what other people will think or say. We worry about making a mistake. We worry about doing the "right" thing. And we worry about losing it all—money, pride, and stature. All of these concerns mask our instincts. And pretty soon, you can't even recognize your true self.

Before we can trust and develop our instincts, we have to know how to recognize that voice from within. The best way to do this, like most things, is to start small. Think about a simple decision you face. It may be choosing a movie or deciding what's for dinner. And this time, let your instincts decide for you. Have fun with the process, but observe it closely. What are you thinking? Then move on to bigger steps, more contentious decisions. What do you feel comfortable with? It could be a business decision (Should I propose this project?) or an approach to parenting (Do I go toe-to-toe with my teen on this one, or let it slide?). Listen to that voice, and trust it.

By 1986, life was very good. I was busy with my rewarding business, and Fred was busy with his. We were a young couple in love, planning our life together. But we had absolutely no idea of the adversity and challenges that lie ahead of us.

MY PLAN TO GET ME CLOSER TO MY DREAM:

Become an ambassador for my country by winning a central beauty pageant.

MY INSTINCTS:

I have a good shot at winning.

THE SEED FOR GOOD:

Learning lessons from achieving women.

Chapter Three

LIFE LESSON:

Act from a Position of Hope, Not Fear

When we make decisions, our choices are often based on either hope or fear. Fear can make us overly cautious and stop us from reaching our true potential. But the power of hope is truly amazing. It is hope that gives us the ability to overcome the odds and achieve what some say can't be done.

When I married a termi-nally ill man, I was governed by hope, not fear. If I had let fear rule, I would have made many different decisions in life—my marriage, my family, and my business success wouldn't have existed. Instead, I operate based on hope, drawing in the positive energy and avoiding the nega-tive. And that approach hasn't let me down yet.

Wedding Bells

Two of Saskatoon's Most Eligibles, Lu-Anne Michelle Gingara and Michael Frederick Mitchell were married in an outdoor ceremony at the Mendel Ranch Saturday afternoon.

— *Star Phoenix*, **August 25, 1986**

On that breezy sunny day in August 1986, none of the 200 or so guests at Fred's mother's ranch knew that behind our bright smiles, we were heartsick. Not long before the greatest day in both of our lives, Fred and I had received a devastating medical diagnosis. The years of breathing difficulties Fred had endured weren't allergies or asthma as doctors had previously thought: Fred was suffering from cystic fibrosis. His lungs were shutting down. The experts gave him, at best, five years to live and told him he wouldn't likely father children.

This news dealt a huge blow to our picture-perfect plans for the future. Children were certainly part of our plan, and I was being told I would be a widow within five years. But the experts didn't know *they* were dealing with Fred Mitchell. He had an absolutely unstoppable spirit. What a great mentor and true hero Fred was. From the moment he received his diagnosis, Fred vowed to beat the odds. He told his doctor he'd be around in 10 years to race up the five flights of stairs to the doctor's office, and he'd beat him. Then we resumed planning our wedding. We placed our name with the local adoption agency soon after. Now I was on the waiting end.

The rather interesting dynamics of Fred's family had become apparent to me when Fred and I were first dating. When Fred picked me up for one of our first dates, I walked out to his car and discovered his mother in the front seat. She was going on the date with us to check me out! I had no idea what we were in for with Fred's family at that time, but his mother made me a bit nervous at first. And it took me a while to realize what a powerful and important family I was becoming involved with. They lived in another world—both socially and financially—but Fred was a kind, down-to-earth person. I felt right at home with him.

A Proud Family Legacy

When Fred and I first met, I was familiar with the company, because my grandfather had been a farmer who sold animals to Intercontinental Packers. Despite what you might think of the meat processing industry, I was never put off by Fred's business. Maybe it's because I was introduced to it through his eyes, and for Fred, the business was all about the people. As Fred did, I have a lot of respect for our people and the skilled work that they do. Many of them live in the area of town I lived in, and I feel like they are "on my level."

Fred was proud of the company's history and began to share it with me. Intercontinental Packers was founded in 1940 by Fred Mendel, a truly mythic character. A brilliant industrialist and wealthy German Jew with meatpacking plants on several continents at one time, Fred Mendel fled the Nazis during World War II, taking his wife and two daughters to New York. He immediately started looking for business opportunities and came across a money-losing manufacturing business in far away Saskatchewan, Canada. I can only imagine Fred Mendel telling his cultured and formerly wealthy wife that they were moving to a small prairie city that was covered in deep snow for half of the year and where temperatures regularly hit 40 below without the windchill. Bravely, the Mendels moved to Saskatoon and started up Intercontinental Packers. Before long, they had opened plants in several other cities.

Fred Mendel was my husband's grandfather and mentor and, by all accounts, an exceptional person. "Papa Mendel," as he was called, established the foundation for Intercontinental's longevity and success with ironclad business ethics—a legacy he handed down to my husband, and via my husband, then to me. His fundamental belief was that if your name is good, everything is good. Given the corporate scandals that have enveloped companies like Enron and WorldCom, that advice is as relevant today as it was more than 60 years ago. When we are told to "go out and make a name for ourselves," I think this is what is meant!

Fred Mendel's daughter, Johanna, met and married a Hollywood actor named Cameron Mitchell. Cameron acted in more than 90 movies and Broadway Shows in his career, including the original *Death of a Salesman* on Broadway and *My Favorite Year*. In *How to Marry a Millionaire*, he romanced Lauren Bacall, who starred along with Marilyn Monroe and Betty Grable. He was perhaps best known for his role as "Buck" in the TV Western *High Chaparral*. Johanna and Cameron lived a glamorous life in Hollywood, Fred told me, socializing with stars like Gary Cooper and Clark Gable. They had four children, but the marriage split up when Fred was nine.

In later years, it was reported that Johanna, as part of bitter family litigation, actually had Cameron jailed for failing to pay family support for her and the children. In time, Cameron and Johanna's eldest son moved to Saskatoon and started working for the family business. Tragically, he died at a very young age several years later. Fred began studies at a university in Arizona. His mother moved to Vancouver with the two youngest children who later pursued acting careers.

During the summers while at school and after graduating from Arizona State University, Fred joined the family business. And he didn't just slide into a cushy executive position—Grampa Mendel made sure his grandson Fred worked several jobs in the plant, giving him valuable insight into and empathy for the jobs his people do day in and day out. Fred even took a commercial meat-cutting course so he could understand that end of the operation. He knew the business inside out, he knew and loved the employees, and they knew and loved him. Fred was named president of Intercontinental Packers at the age of 29. He had met and married a girl from university, but the marriage had dissolved. We met ten years later.

LOCAL BEAUTY QUEEN
MARRIES LEADING SCION

That headline from a local magazine captures how Fred's family probably viewed me—a young beauty queen from the boonies. From the very beginning, I felt like I got a pretty cool reception from Fred's mother, brother, and sister. His aristocratic mother, although likable, was outspoken and was especially critical, making derogatory comments to me about my clothing and my table manners at dinners in her home at the ranch. I was hurt, but I took it in stride. What else could I do? Fred used to say to me that it wouldn't matter what I did or said; his family thought I didn't have the right "pedigree" to marry him. To his mother's credit, she did put on a wonderful party for our wedding, but his mother would strategically place photos of Fred's ex-wife around her home when we would come to visit. Fred would pull leaves off her trees and shove them between the frame and the photo. We would watch them shrivel over time, then he would replace them. It became our little joke. I said, "I feel like I am always being judged." "You are," he would respond. He was right.

It seemed obvious to me that Fred's mother thought I was a fortune hunter, because prior to our marriage, Fred asked me to sign an ironclad prenuptial agreement. The thick "pre-nup" essentially ensured I would gain no stake in the family business. I was stunned when Fred put this document in front of me and asked me to sign it. He pleaded with me, saying his mother insisted on it. I didn't understand, and it just didn't feel right to me. So, I put him off gently. Fred explained that to make it legal, I had to consult with a lawyer.

When I showed the agreement to a lawyer, he interpreted it: "Someone in this family wants you under their thumb," the lawyer explained placing his thumb down squarely on his desk. "You must understand that you would be married in name only." There were some tears and some arguments, but in the end I relented and signed it. There was no negotiation, no argument from me—just surrender. I could see that it was important to Fred. And I was focusing on our marriage, not a potential marriage breakdown. I didn't want anything anyway, just his love. Then we put the agreement in a safety deposit box and never spoke of it again.

Despite the shock of being presented with a pre-nup, which was totally foreign to me, I still believed that Fred was an exceedingly decent man who would stand by me, I would stand by him, and we would never let each other down. As a result of the agreement, I was never an employee of Intercontinental Packers and had no ownership involvement with the company or its assets until 1997 when Fred and I together acquired the pork division as part of the settlement with the rest of his family. For the first ten years of our marriage, I really owned nothing on my own. Because of his health diagnosis and rapidly deteriorating condition in the first years of our marriage, Fred had no personal life insurance other than his coverage through the company. And I had no career. I became his caregiver and had to be ready to care for him 24/7. If I was marrying him for his money and a luxurious, pampered life, I sure messed up!

Defying the Odds

If you've beaten the odds once, you know it can be done. I learned this when we faced Fred's illness head-on. I was only 25 and starting an exciting new life with the man I loved. He was the 39-year-old longtime swinging bachelor, finally ready to settle down. And then—whack! Fred and I were hit with a cosmic two-by-four. After an extensive check-up at the Mayo Clinic in Rochester Minnesota, the doctors told us he had a rare form of cystic fibrosis. They said he was in the "gray zone" because he didn't have the usual stomach problems so common to these cases, and he was old! People with CF usually die by the age of 26. The outlook wasn't good. But Fred's stellar reaction taught me a lot about what you do when adversity strikes. He would say, "Honey, we've just got to find a solution." And it became apparent that a lung transplant was the only possible solution. We started exploring our options.

One transplant program wanted nothing to do with us. Fred was considered to be too sick, and they went so far as to say they didn't like his attitude. Even at this worst point, he saw himself as whole and healed, and they thought he was quite nuts! We discovered that lungs are sometimes transplanted with hearts—the new lungs function better when they come as a package deal with a heart so far as rejection goes. We were now looking for a heart/double lung transplant. Finally, we found a program that would accept us. The Stanford Medical Center in Palo Alto, California accepted Fred into the transplant program there and because he was an American citizen, born and raised in Los Angeles, the transplant was funded under a federal grant program out of Washington! He was essentially a guinea pig and happy to oblige.

Meanwhile, Fred's health was in serious decline. It was sometimes very difficult for him to breathe, and he was losing weight rapidly. His skin became ruddy, and he was weak. I learned how to precision-pound on his chest to clear his lungs while he lay on a slant board, a therapy used in these cases. I also became involved in helping him take his medications and was with him at all his doctors' appointments. We kept him out of hospitals as much as possible because of risk of secondary infections. But when we had to enter, he would wear a mask. There was a lot of nursing to be done at home. It was quite ironic to find myself in that role because I always said that the one job I'd never want is to be a nurse! I feel faint at the thought of needles or the sight of blood. Well, I had a lot of nursing ahead of me. His mother called several times, disappointed in me and not confident that he was being looked after properly. "He was never sick a day in his life before he met you," she once told me. I was devastated.

THIS GUY'S NOT GOING TO MAKE IT

About a year after our marriage, I was delighted to discover I was pregnant. During my pleasant pregnancy, we spent some time in Hawaii. The climate was good for Fred, and we loved the ocean. On one trip, Fred had to be hospitalized for nearly two months. While he was mildly sedated in the hospital, he overheard a nurse say about him: "This guy's not going to make it. Why don't we have someone in here that we can help? He's just using up a bed." At that very moment, Fred's attitude changed. When I came into the hospital that afternoon, he said in a crackling voice, one runaway tear trickling down his cheek: "Honey, if modern medicine can't help me, God will. I am ready to receive a miracle."

Until then, Fred didn't have a strong faith. Many times, he felt cheated on every level, including spiritually. But when he put his complete trust in a Higher Power and surrendered his earthly logic, good things began to happen: "miracles." Fred read many inspiring books. It comes back to the proven belief that you become like those who surround you. And we embraced the philosophy that if you surround yourself with people who throw pity parties for you or make you stop believing in yourself and your mission, your strength will just evaporate. Spend your precious time with people who inspire you to achieve great things in life. Many wonderful teachers are a huge part of the success I have enjoyed.

Our First Miracle: Freddie, Jr.

Fred and I saw my amazing pregnancy as a very positive sign that we could beat the odds regarding his illness. They said it couldn't be done—so what! Freddie, Jr. was born in 1988, a beautiful healthy nine-pound boy, 100 years after Fred Mendel's birth in 1888. Sometimes I watch home videos that we took when Freddie was a baby. Fred was a completely doting dad, constantly talking to the baby whom he nicknamed "Champ" and clowning around. While I was pregnant, we read *Kindergarten Is Too Late* by Masaru Ibuka, one of the founders of Sony. It was valuable to apply some of the ideas about listening to classical music and talking to the baby in the womb! As someone who grew up with a dad who left the family for another woman when he was a boy, Fred vowed to be an involved, loving father and husband. And he was. What a happy time it was even amid the uncertainty. But it didn't last for long.

Fred became so ill that he couldn't even hold Champ. He was living in our sunroom, which we kept heated to 98.6 degrees, and he still felt chilled. I would go in there three times a day to beat his chest to help him breathe between nursing Freddie, who had become colicky; and playing catch-up with laundry, dinner, and cleaning. I got painful persistent migraine headaches from the extreme temperature and hectic schedule. One night, as I was nursing Freddie, Jr. on my left breast in bed, I felt something warm and wet on my right shoulder. Fred's failing lungs were hemorrhaging—there was blood all over our bed and us. I immediately called 911. Semi-conscious and gushing blood, he was rushed to hospital in an ambulance. They thought it was over, but Fred refused to hear that. He had a job to do.

As soon as he was well enough to travel, we flew to California. We needed a private plane because he could not fly commercial and risk catching something from someone else—just one cough could do it. At that point, a buzz started up in our city. People had seen a frail and skinny Fred, clutching an IV pole, leaning on his wife, and boarding a plane. Rumors started flying that he had AIDS. But rumors were the least of our worries. Humbled beyond words and clinging to each other for dear life, we went to the Stanford Medical Center and started praying for a miracle.

MY PLAN TO GET ME CLOSER TO MY DREAM:
Marry Fred and start a family.

MY INSTINCTS:
This is a man who will always stand by me.

THE SEED FOR GOOD:
Firsthand experience with miracles.

Chapter Four

LIFE LESSON:

Don't Give in to Long Odds

Sometimes, it seems that the world is full of overly careful people who like to tell you why something can't be achieved. And, yes, quite often the odds are against us—whether it's sustaining a marriage (more than half fail), starting a business (a similarly high failure rate), or overcoming an illness (the doctors are great at providing scary percentages).

Imagine what our world would be like if everyone bowed to the odds, not even trying to defy them. We would have no entrepreneurs, no dreamers, and no miracles. I've seen enough miracles in my life to believe that the odds should be considered just another obstacle to overcome. With hope, faith, and perseverance, you can overcome the odds. Believe it.

My son's brave battle for life—
and the miracle that saved him.

— Cameron Mitchell's article in the
National Enquirer, January 28, 1992

Once we got to *California*, all we could do was wait for an organ donor. It was a tough time—Fred was deathly ill, and we were both anxious. We rented a home in Hillsborough, California, just outside of San Francisco while we waited for his transplant. Fred was emaciated and so weak that he could hardly walk. His skin became very ruddy and at nights, we would wake to his nightmares and sweats. I would rock him and hum a tune as I stroked his forehead, praying constantly. The doctors said that in his worsening condition, Fred had just weeks to live: two weeks to be exact. To get an organ donor who had a healthy heart and lungs, the right tissue, and a blood match was like winning the ultimate lottery. But we did—we got an exact match within two weeks.

One day, we got a babysitter for Freddie, who was two years old at the time and were enjoying going on our first date together in ages—lunch in San Francisco. It was the first time that Fred was off his intravenous and outside moving around freely. On the way to lunch, I had an overwhelming urge to call home. Fred was wearing a pager, which would go off if the hospital found a transplant match. "Why interrupt our day?" he asked, and an argument ensued. But I persisted and defiantly picked up the car phone anyway.

The lesson we learned that day was to trust instincts over pagers every time.

When our babysitter answered the call, she was frantic: The hospital had been calling non-stop (turns out the pager was broken and the car phone was out of range just a short time earlier). A perfect match had been found for Fred's transplant. He had to return to the hospital and it was important that he didn't eat. If we had continued to San Francisco for lunch, he quite likely wouldn't have been able to have the transplant. The lesson we learned that day was to trust instincts over pagers every time—especially a woman's instinct in this case.

MITCHELL MIRACLE: "I DIDN'T WANT TO DIE"

Fred later told me that the last thing he remembered before going under for his transplant operation as he was being wheeled in was that the operating room looked a bit like the cut and kill floor at his family's meatpacking plant. And he was right. The equipment that surgeons use for this type of surgery is a lot like the equipment meatpackers use to crack the chest cavities on cows and pigs. When the anesthetic hit, Fred told me he hallucinated and thought the doctors were all cows with masks on saying to him: "Now it's your turn, buddy!" He was so glad to wake up again.

At one point during Fred's operation, I saw a surgeon come out of the operating room with a small Coleman cooler. I had a small jolt when I realized what it was—my husband's heart being taken to another operating room to be transplanted. Fred was what is termed a "domino"—in addition to receiving a new heart and lungs, he donated his healthy heart to a recipient. A 52-year-old woman with a heart condition was the recipient of Fred's strong heart, which had been compensating for two burnt out lungs. Fred later joked that I was the only woman in the world who literally saw her husband give his heart to another woman. He also joked about leaving his heart in San Francisco. That was vintage Fred—finding humor and lightening every moment in almost any situation no matter how bleak.

The heart/double lung transplant was a success. Even the *National Enquirer* said so! One day, I was at a corner store in Palm Springs picking up a few groceries. Imagine my surprise when, while browsing the cover of the latest tabloid, I see Liz Taylor, Larry Fortensky, and inside—Fred Mitchell! I scooped up all the copies in that store and rushed home to read it. I thought, *Oh, my goodness, did I marry a space alien? What's going on?* It was a heartwarming story, told from the point of view of Fred's father, the longtime Hollywood actor. Fred's brother, Chip, was a faithful visitor during the time of Fred's transplant, and his other family members were on the phone with him at the hospital. I was never called to the phone. I stayed in the waiting room in a blur. Fred's family members visited occasionally later. It was a long, slow recovery. There was the worry of organ rejection for several months, but Fred was alive and he had a healthy new set of lungs. A new light shone from his hazel eyes. We had beaten the odds—again!

MORE THAN A GAME

During Fred's long recovery from the transplant surgery, I faced several challenges. I was single parenting a toddler and making endless trips to the hospital to visit with Fred and help with his rehabilitation. Once the crisis passed and it was clear that Fred was returning to good health, I began to get a bit restless. Those were long, lonely days, and sometimes I longed to escape. I cried a river— I am sure the San Francisco Bay rose to new levels with the flood from my aching heart! I planted some seeds. I put all that water to good use and I created my own escape, a board game called "Save the Planet."

The idea for "Save the Planet" came from my fervent environmentalism. I wondered how I could create a greener planet while also enjoying a new creative outlet for myself. I realize now that creating this game was an important coping mechanism for me in the aftermath of such a grueling time.

You don't always have to answer when opportunity knocks.

Gradually, the game took shape. I designed it for children so families could play it together and learn about conservation and ecology. Once I had the concept, I started working with a designer who created a colorful board for the game and an attractive outer box.

One day, while visiting Fred at the Stanford Medical Center, I met a man whose wife was waiting for a transplant. The man was Dennis Hayes, founder of Earth Day. He took one of my games, later telling me in a lovely letter how much he and his staff enjoyed it. "Save the Planet" even garnered me some attention among "the ladies who lunch" in Beverly Hills. When I had lunch with some high-profile Hollywood wives to promote my game and Kids for Saving Earth, a nonprofit organization for which I served as the volunteer National Advisor for North America, our picture ended up on the cover of *Beverly Hills Today*.

I was in discussion with a large toy maker to market "Save the Planet" on a national scale when Fred's family problems escalated. I shifted my priorities and put my game on hold. You don't always have to answer when opportunity knocks. It can be a knee-jerk reaction instead of a thoughtful decision. Sometimes, the opportunity is there but the timing is wrong. Now, instead of wondering, "What if?" I see "Save the Planet" as another seed for good that came out of Fred's health challenges.

Our world needs a new "heart and lungs" (oceans and forests), I thought, and so did Fred. It all starts with me—the best I can do—and perhaps, it will catch on. How wonderful!

CAN YOU TEACH ME TO DO THAT?

Sometimes the most unexpected actions can break down walls between people. I discovered this when Fred and I attended the Beverly Hills Policemen's Ball one year with our dear friends Sooky and Sam Goldman. You can imagine the scene—celebrities, actors, studio executives, and the like, all dressed to the nines. One reason we attended was to see the evening's entertainment, The Pointer Sisters, but the main reason was

> *Sometimes the most unexpected actions can break down walls between people.*

to be with Sooky who was the beautiful spirit of the region. She was one of the organizers and a real angel on earth.

The Pointer Sisters were phenomenal! It was a fabulous show, and during the applause after one song, I instinctively started whistling—one of those loud whistles, two fingers on either side of the mouth. I watched my brother play hockey all winter long as a child and learned a whistle that could carry across the largest hockey rink; I was a real "rink rat" in my day.

When I let loose at this Beverly Hills party, I raised a few eyebrows, but I was as delighted as I could be. Afterward, a dignified older woman motioned me over. *Uh oh*, I thought, *she's going to put me in my place.* Instead, she smiled and said, "Can you teach me how to do that, dahling?" It was a great icebreaker and a reminder that you just shouldn't take life too seriously and never judge. This sweet Beverly Hills gal had a little light go on inside her at the party when the girl in the red strapless silk gown whistled and cut loose.

YOUR HUSBAND WILL NEVER FATHER ANOTHER CHILD

After Fred's transplant, the doctors made it quite clear that the likelihood of Fred fathering another child was very slim. That hadn't changed. We felt strongly about having a sibling for Freddie, so we registered with the local adoption agency. It wasn't long before we got the happy news: a young, single pregnant girl in the San Francisco area was looking for parents for her child. Several months later, we were holding our new son Ryan. With laughing eyes and gorgeous curly blonde hair, we loved him at first sight. We were just adjusting to life with a baby when I got one of the biggest shocks of my life: I was pregnant! Once again, Fred had defied the odds. He would indeed father another biological child.

It was during this time that Fred's company opened a facility in Commerce, California, just outside Los Angeles, to launch his company's products into the massive West Coast market. Fred had grown up in Pacific Palisades as an avid surfer and might have ended up an oceanographer were it not for the lure of the family business. With our rapidly growing family, we needed a real home. And we found it: a beautiful estate in the Old Las Palmas neighborhood of Palm Springs. Formerly owned by the famous hotelier Kirk Kerkorian, our new home had towering palm trees, a large pool, and full garden, complete with several fresh fruit trees and my personal favorite birds of paradise. It was just down the street from Granny Mendel's former home and near Fred's mother's condo. It was an ideal location, but there was one catch: I would have absolutely no ownership of it.

This significant detail was a surprise to me. I was pregnant with our daughter, severely anemic and very tired when Fred walked in with some documents for me to sign. To qualify for an interest-free mortgage from his company, he explained, he had to be the sole owner of the property. When I realized that Fred was asking me to sign away ownership of our new home, I stood my very pregnant self up, picked up baby Ryan on one hip and my purse, took Freddie, Jr. by the hand, and started walking out the door.

We were staying at the Miramar Hotel in Santa Monica at the time. I silently walked out the door and headed for the elevator. Fred chased me down the hall and into the elevator, wondering what I was doing. In fact, I had it in my mind to ask the concierge for the address of the local women's shelter. Fred got very agitated when he saw how serious I was. In our entire married life, this was the closest I came to leaving him. In the elevator, I listened while Fred explained that once we paid off the mortgage, we would own the house together.

Just as I did with the prenuptial agreement, I chose to trust Fred about this. I hated the idea of his mother or the family business trying to pull strings in our lives, but I ultimately understood that this was out of Fred's control. When they saw the tears in their father's eyes, the children looked at us with fear and desperation. We returned to the hotel room, and I signed the papers. Then we just put it behind us and moved into our new home with enthusiasm and joy.

It's important to recognize the position I was in at this time. I had two small children and another on the way. I had a husband whose health history precluded him from being eligible for life insurance. My prenuptial agreement meant I was entitled to nothing from his business. I owned nothing. If Fred had died, I would have been destitute. But that simply wasn't my focus at the time. I was reveling in my children, each of them a miracle and a great gift. I took my responsibility as a parent and wife very seriously. I had energy and creativity galore. I knew I was going to build something—maybe another game, maybe another beauty spa, maybe a talk show again one day—I didn't know what, but I was full of enthusiasm for the opportunities that lie ahead.

GLOOM GIVES WAY TO HOPE AFTER TRANSPLANT SURGERY

The odds were stacked high against Fred living a healthy, vigorous life. But with a bit of luck, modern technology, and a lot of faith, Fred beat those odds for many happy years. He returned to work with a new vigor and a new attitude. His transplant experience had strengthened his faith, and he was quite open about his belief in doing God's work on earth. Always a strong supporter of his employees, Fred adopted a more positive approach to all aspects of doing business. As he said, "I used to try to see through people. Now I try to see people through." Building the business was an important part of his healing.

> *I used to try to see through people. Now I try to see people through.*

Fred truly believed he had been given a new lease on life. We were both growing spiritually, thanks to some awesome mentors. My journey of learning began in earnest during those years in California. When Fred was still in the hospital post-transplant, sometimes I just had to get out of there, away from the negative energy.

One day, I read about a woman who was coming to San Francisco to speak. I was in the audience, baby Freddie at my side. Her message—that prosperity is within you—really resonated with me. Always an avid reader, I began expanding my repertoire to inspirational authors and speakers. I was a sponge, soaking up the information, and taking it back to Fred. We both learned so much from Reverend Robert Schuller, a follower of Norman Vincent Peale, as we were. Fred appeared on the *Hour of Power* TV program after his transplant, talking about how his faith sustained him through this trying experience. Years later, I would also be interviewed on that enormously popular and powerful

> *We didn't realize it at the time, but we were being prepared for the challenges that lie ahead.*

program. For years, I was the girl in the audience silently whistling my best whistle for my mentors and teachers—inside my mind—taking notes and asking questions. I had no idea where this learning would take me.

We didn't realize it at the time, but we were being prepared for the challenges that lie ahead. Our mentors were preparing us for the challenges that lie ahead. We would need all their wisdom, positive energy, and possibility thinking to weather some very stormy seas.

MY PLAN TO GET ME CLOSER TO MY DREAM:

Standing by my husband despite tough times.

MY INSTINCTS:

Calling home on our day out to discover a transplant was imminent.

THE SEED FOR GOOD:

Fred's recovery and "rebirth," the growth of our family.

Chapter Five

LIFE LESSON:

Define Your Dream

Ask someone what their dream is, and they might say they want to be rich and happy. But what's "rich" and what's "happy"? Would you know if you were there? Is "rich" dollars and cents, or is it your health? Is it a combination? Is happiness out there or in you? You must figure it out and make it part of your plan.

You can't map out your direction unless you have a very specific destination. You need to be able to see yourself achieving your goal. While some of us instinctively know what our dream is, others have to take the time to define what it is (or isn't). Once you have that goal, the fun part starts: making that dream a reality.

High noon in Saskatoon.

— *Maclean's*, April 29, 1996

During the time of Fred's transplant and convalescence, his mother, sister, and brother became more involved in the family business. For a long time, Fred, as President, had been the family member who was most significantly involved in the day-to-day operations of Intercontinental Packers. Fred would report to his mother, Johanna Mitchell. Johanna had assumed control of the company after Grampa Mendel's death but only following a protracted and bitter legal battle with her own sister.

Fred had started working at Intercontinental Packers during the summer when he was still in school, and then full time after graduating from college, and had been President since he was 29. His brother and sister pursued careers in acting.

Some things changed in the family dynamics during Fred's illness—his mother and siblings started to take a far more active role in the business. They were very helpful in their own way when Fred was ill. But after he returned to work full time, disagreements arose among the family members concerning the business. Before long, Fred realized his mother and siblings were battling him for control; they could not agree on the direction of the company. Tensions rose and soon the family members found themselves unable to work together. "Four of us cannot take the reins and ride a horse, even if it is a thoroughbred," Fred said at the time.

Packing Plant Chief Resigns; Cites "Unacceptable Changes"

The simmering family tensions hit the boiling point over the issue of a proposed plant closure. Fred was adamant that the plant in Vancouver, British Columbia was creating inefficiencies for the company as a whole and that the same should be shut down. As Fred explained to me later, his siblings and mother disagreed and outvoted him thereby, in Fred's view, effectively undercutting his authority. Realizing that he was unable to lead the company the way he once did as its President and CEO the way he thought it should be run, Fred announced, "I won't be the captain of the Titanic." And he left. After more than 30 years with the company and 18 years as President and CEO, Fred launched a lawsuit for constructive dismissal. It wasn't long before we got his family's response: They countersued. The legal battle had begun. As Fred said, "There needs to be a divorce alright, honey. But it's not between us—it's between me and my family." He was devastated but strong.

Years later, I was told that when the Mitchell family feud began (and without my knowledge), Fred had instructed his lawyer to have his rights under our "pre-nup" agreement terminated so that matrimonial property law would apply to our relationship. Fred advised his lawyer that, given the strength of the love between us, there would never be an issue. I am glad to say that, as usual, he was right.

All families have problems, a friend once assured me; it's just that most family problems aren't played out in the headlines. The Mitchell family feud was tantalizing fodder for the headline writers. Fred and I were accused of living "high off the hog" (they can't resist a good pun), and they wrote endlessly about the "family beef." It might have been fun to write about, but it was no fun to live through.

Meanwhile, the legal battle continued. There were gag orders, injunctions, and sealing of court files. It soon became clear that this was not going to be settled quickly or amicably. It was truly ugly and demeaning. The impact of this highly public family feud was felt by all of us, even our children. I'll never forget my son Freddie coming home from school in tears after being teased about the latest headline in the newspaper. No child should have to endure that. Fortunately, his father and I knew the power of hugs and unconditional love. We sure had an abundance of both in our home and hearts.

MITCHELLS SELL PALM SPRINGS HOME

In 1994, Fred and I hit rock bottom financially. We were living in a gray used Chevy van with three small children and three dogs. We faced the very real prospect of risking it all—and losing. But we held on. Some dear people in this world put out their hands to help us in any way they could, not caring who would "win," so to speak.

As the family feud escalated, there came a time when Fred and I could have just walked away. The lawyers' bills were mounting, and our hopes were flagging. But I can honestly say we never seriously considered giving up the fight. Finally, we were up against the wall financially: We had to cash in virtually everything we owned to pay legal bills. Fred's mortgage was called, and we quickly sold our beautiful estate in Palm Springs in a fire sale, as well our cars, including a Porsche show car and a Cadillac. All we had left was our beaten up 1992 Chevy run-around van. It was rickety, but roomy, so we packed in the kids—then ages 6, 3, and 2—plus our two Rottweilers, Bunny and Clyde; and toy poodle, Babykins, and like gypsies, headed north. The van was full of baby seats and bottles, dog food, and diapers—it reeked of baby and dog.

Driving first through Las Vegas and then across the border, we went to Calgary, trying to find consulting work for Fred (not many companies were keen to hire a heart/double lung transplant recipient pulling up with this circus act caravan, no matter how brilliant!).

The winners in life are those who dare to dream ...and they dare to dream big dreams.

Believe it or not, I have some happy memories from that time—playing with my precious babies, walking my dogs, and feeling the sense of adventure of being on a road trip. Both Fred and I had a strong faith that this wasn't forever, that "this too shall pass." Finally we hit terra firma—my mother's apartment at Clinskill Manor—a seniors' residence in Saskatoon. She moved in with my brother and his family so we had a home. But that didn't last long. Our family of five eventually got kicked out of the seniors' residence for being too young. That was a nice thing to know because we felt old and beat up, tired, and sick. Although we did not fit on the outside, we sure felt the part.

Finally, Fred sold a cherished gift to him from Granny Mendel, a painting by the famous artist Emily Carr. Although he was reluctant to let it go, Fred realized that our family needed a home. The funds from the sale of that painting provided us with almost enough money for a down payment. With a little smart negotiating, we bought a beautiful new home in Saskatoon, a white elephant for the developer, not at all sure how we were going to pay the mortgage coming due one day. We rented with a promise. It was a turbulent time. But what kept us sane and united were our passion for our dream and our strong love for each other, our children, and our company dreams.

DARING TO DREAM BIG DREAMS

The winners in life are those who dare to dream . . . and they dare to dream big dreams. I guess my independent streak surfaced early. In kindergarten, I adopted the distinctive spelling of LuAn. My teacher discouraged this kind of thinking saying, "Sometimes you just have to accept your lot in life." Well you know what—I didn't believe that then, and I still don't believe that now.

Try to be specific about your dream. It's a good idea to close your eyes and see yourself there. What does it look like when you've achieved the dream? Is your dream about reaching a certain level of success in business? Enjoying the freedom of running your own business? Or is it about living in a certain place or achieving a more personal goal? Make your visual image as precise as possible so you can clearly see yourself where you want to be. Are there smells you would smell, tastes you would taste, and sounds you would hear? Is it realistic—can it be done in the timeframe? Make it real.

> *Make your visual image as precise as possible so you can clearly see yourself where you want to be.*

Think about something you really want to achieve. Be as specific as you can. For instance, when Fred and I were developing our original blueprint for Mitchell's, we wanted to get the company pumping along so well that anyone who suggested shutting it down would have to be nuts. It was the ultimate survivor game, but it was also a very clearly defined goal. It was a vision we could grab on to— we could feel it. From that original vision—a vibrant meat processing business that had the capacity to meet our customers' needs—we then started creating a business plan. By the time we were finished, it filled several binders. But the most important thing we did was to define our goal clearly and make the commitment to each other that we would stand strong together on the journey toward the goal.

PUTTING THE DREAM ON HOLD

As important as it is to remain committed to your dream, sometimes it's more important to know when to switch gears. There have been several times in my life when I've had to put my dreams aside. One of those times was when we were living in Palm Springs in the early 1990s.

> *As important as it is to remain committed to your dream, sometimes it's more important to know when to switch gears.*

Fred's health was vastly improved after the transplant, and we were starting to settle into a normal family life. I finally had a bit of time to pursue one of my interests: journalism. I had done some freelance writing in Canada before my marriage and loved it. I called one of the local lifestyle magazines, *Palm Springs Life*, and suggested a story about the area's top personal trainers. They accepted and the story was lots of fun—a big spread in the magazine with the personal trainers dressed as superheroes.

My career was beginning to take off. On the cover of *Palm Springs Life* that issue were Frank and Barbara Sinatra, two people I admired and loved. Then I had an opportunity for a small part on the hit TV program, *Melrose Place*, which was a wonderful experience. Next came an offer to submit a resume to help out on a new pilot called *Models Inc.* for Fox.

Wow, I just couldn't believe it! Just as my life finally opened up a few opportunities, Fred's was heading into a tailspin. I could see it was time to put my aspirations aside in response to my husband's desperate plea for help—not forever, but certainly for the time being. Before long, we were packing the family into the van and heading north to tend to business. I always thought I would return one day and then it would be set right!

> *Too many people go through life with their emergency brake tightly on. They're afraid that if they take the brake off, they'll go too fast, lose control, and get hurt.*

GETTING COMFORTABLE WITH RISK

Too many people go through life with their emergency brake tightly on. They're afraid that if they take the brake off, they'll go too fast, lose control, and get hurt. We are too scared to cut loose from conformity—like the moment I lost myself and whistled at a black tie ball because I love the Pointer Sisters. Our fears can get out of control and can run our life. The important thing is to realize that while our fears will always be there, they don't have to paralyze us; we can learn to move forward. And if we just go out and

> *While our fears will always be there, they don't have to paralyze us—we can learn to move forward.*

"do it" often enough, like the Nike ad says, the fear disappears. It can even become a force for good pushing us on.

The fact is that if you take risks, you'll likely make a few mistakes—maybe even fall down now and then. But innovation and success can only come from someone with the creativity and courage to try, fail, learn from their failure, and try again. There really is no failure, except the failure to try if you are on a valuable mission. We must stop focusing on life's errors, other people's inadequacies, and self-recrimination—all of which is pointless. Instead, recognize your strengths and build on them. Difficulties are only there as forces to use to our advantage; we have to "figure it out."

When I was growing up, I got used to hearing, "If it was so easy, someone would have done it by now." Sound familiar? Creativity was frowned upon as not being able to "fit in" or failure to "follow the leader"—they're not for everyone. It's all been done before, or it's too difficult. Haven't you heard those negative messages before?

You don't need to consult and get agreement from 80 of your best buddies for the really important decisions in life. Did you know the best advice already lies within you?

But as I grew up, I kept asking myself, "Why are all the leaders usually men?" It seems to be a crazy world comprised of a big "ole boys club" of power brokers all right or a new generation of "keep 'em pregnant and in the kitchen" types! Why is it wrong for women to try new ideas, to think of new solutions, be world leaders—take it "out there" to blaze new trails? And I haven't found a good reason yet.

Women leaders are sometimes characterized as being too

masculine or plain old frustrated. I am neither; I am quite balanced, but still I am not afraid to state my case. In a recent meeting with my "all men and me" ratio, one of the guys thought it was a good time to tell a meatpacker joke. "Hey, LuAn, know why they call it 'PMS'? Because mad cow disease was already taken!" Ha, ha! Oh yeah, I've had my share.

What Are You Willing to Risk?

Certainly, each of us has our own level of comfort with risk. The important thing is to define how much risk you are willing to take. There are not too many risks that will imperil our lives. Walking the high wire without a net can be foolish and dangerous. What is it that you're really risking? Your home? Your car? Security? Health? A lawsuit perhaps? Or maybe it's just a little thing like the possible embarrassment of trying and failing. In fact, not trying at all is failure for sure.

Start by tuning out the other voices. You don't need to consult and get agreement from 80 of your best buddies for the really important decisions in life. Did you know the best advice already lies within you? Think about what you are working toward and what you are willing to gamble—even sacrifice in your life. A lot of what we have in life is just stuff, sometimes even clutter. Like

> We all have to figure out what are the things in life that are precious to us.

pack rats, each of us has things we aren't willing to give up or even lend periodically.

I'm blessed today to live a comfortable life, but I sometimes surprise people with my choice of jewelry. You might find me at a black tie event dressed in an elegant evening gown and sporting a necklace my creative and artistic son Freddie gave me with love many years ago. The necklace is made of dried colored pasta, plastic beads, and rolled up newspaper. Many gifts are given with love. But this one was also *made* with love when Freddie was in kindergarten in Palm Springs. Take any pricey bauble in my jewelry box, but don't touch my precious pasta necklace. That's irreplaceable—we can't turn back the hands of time. We all have to figure out what are the things in life that are precious to us. I had to consider hocking my diamond wedding ring once but never my kindergarten jewel. No one would have given me the time of day, much less money for my beautiful piece. No one knows its value—that's between my son and me.

> *Think about what you are working toward and what you are willing to gamble—even sacrifice in your life.*

The rest of the stuff in my lock box is just show-off stuff, and you must have faith that you can live happily without it. Trust your instincts. Then start looking around for opportunities and start taking risks, putting it on the line sometimes if you must. That's how big dreams come true.

A Daring Tradition

Our company was founded by a risk-taker. In 1940, Fred Mendel fled Nazi Germany, leaving most of his fortune behind. Arriving in New York City, he discovered there was a business for sale in a little town in the prairie provinces of Canada that would lend itself to becoming a meatpacking business. It was the only business he knew and wanted to start in the new world. The business was ailing (some people thought the building was cursed), my late husband told me. His grandfather was about 52, spoke little English, had a heart condition, and was heading to a small flat city with a harsh climate where he knew no one. That's what I'd call having the odds stacked against you! But he took that risk. And he succeeded, helping countless people along the way.

MITCHELL KNOWN FOR HIS UNSTOPPABLE SPIRIT

The legal battles with his family were heartbreaking for Fred. He was not a man who enjoyed adversarial relationships. He was a pleasant, easygoing man, but he had huge inner strength. He wasn't prepared to be separated from this company and its people he loved so deeply. Throughout this adversity, amazingly, he maintained his positive spirit. When something would come up, Fred would say, "What problem?" It used to drive me crazy. I thought it what we should be worrying about was so obvious. But Fred would say, "Oh, that. That just means we shouldn't go that way. It means something better is coming. We need to regroup and revisit."

You can hash over injustices and wrongdoings endlessly, but it's much more productive to move on and look for the next opportunity or the next seed for good.

His attitude taught me a lot: It taught me that you can hash over injustices and wrongdoings endlessly, but it's much more productive to move on and look for the next opportunity or the next seed for good. Whether it's office politics, a sales situation or family relations, don't get mired in the mud. Rise above and move on to the next great thing that is waiting for you.

It must have come as a surprise to some people that our marriage not only endured but *flourished* during these trying times. Fred once told a member of his family, and it was witnessed by others and myself: "You've done everything in your power to dry me up financially so

my wife would leave me. But she'd never leave me." And he was right;
I would never throw him to the sharks. He treated me like a lady,
and I returned the favor to my man. By late 1996, our personal financial crisis was about to end. Our corporate financial challenges,
however, were just beginning. Time to mount the champion and ride.
We were "off to the races."

MY PLAN TO GET ME CLOSER TO MY DREAM:

Help Fred gain control of the family's pork processing business and build our new company into a strong force to save
our people and their jobs.

MY INSTINCTS:

It's worth risking it all for our new company and its future.

THE SEED FOR GOOD:

Fred and my first business partnership blossom.

Chapter Six

LIFE LESSON:

Seek Alliances to Support Your Dream

When you're up against the wall, you start to think creatively. When our company was in dire financial straits, we started to look for allies. And we found them in the most unlikely places. Our company exists today in part because of alliances with a major competitor and some "Old Boys' Club" types as well as an investor group from Asia.

Look to friends and support-ers for alliances, but also open your eyes to other possibilities, no matter how improbable. But make sure they are a match with both your long-range goals and your ultimate short-term goals. You may not plan to do lunch together but it is not about lunch; it's about what you bring to the table and creating win-win situations. And ultimately, it's about achieving your dream.

Mitchell settles beef
with family.

— *Star Phoenix*, **October 30, 1996**

While they were battling each other in court, Fred and his family still spoke occasionally. But the damage had been done, and I could see that Fred's relationship with some members of his family had turned bitter. We began receiving strange phone calls at our home and were sufficiently concerned that we began recording some of them. One of the calls that we recorded was so frightening that we decided to go to the police and ask that charges be pressed. In due course, Fred's sister was charged with uttering threats against me.

While all this was going on, I decided I couldn't live in fear. I loved Fred, but I didn't want to be the sacrificial lamb. I began taking karate courses, both as a way of defending myself and as an outlet for my energy. I had a fabulous instructor who taught me a lot in a short time. I particularly remember one mindbender that he provided.

"In your mind, put an owl in a cage," he said. "This is a cage with solid bars, an impenetrable lock and a solid bottom and top. How can you get the owl out of the cage? There is a way—you find it."

He left us with this question until our next class a week later.

I pondered his question all week and was stumped. So was the rest of the class, I discovered to my relief when we met again.

"The answer is simple," our instructor said. "You put the owl in the cage in your mind. You took suggested thoughts from me and made them real; you can dismiss them at any time you wish. Take him out again in your mind."

I believe in visualizing what we want to be in all its splendor.

I learned the important lesson that sometimes we discount the power of our minds to make things happen. We lock ourselves in the owl cage and throw away the key. I believe in visualizing what we want to be in all its splendor. In my imagination, I see wonderful things coming to the people I love and others, too—even those whom I'm not so sure about.

I have also forgiven every member of Fred's family. My journey and theirs have been very different. But his mother gave him life, and I shall thank her forever for that. I believe in letting people off the hook, so to speak. I harbor no resentment, and I work hard on praying for his brother's and sister's best dreams coming true for highest good and the good of the world.

The way I see it, my freedom ends where another person's nose begins. God knows, so to win the game, let him run the ball. I see peace in my life. And I have faith that if I walk with God, this will come to pass.

THE FAMILY DECIDED IT WAS IN EVERYONE'S BEST INTERESTS TO RESOLVE THESE ISSUES

Before Fred's sister's case was heard in court, Fred and his family reached an out-of-court settlement. His mother, sister, and brother got ownership of the company's beef packing plant. Fred and I got ownership of the pork processing operations of the company. As part of the agreement, all litigation between the family members was dropped. The family feud was officially over. Soon thereafter, the charges against Fred's sister were dropped.

There was no turning back now, so we did the only thing we could do: We got to work.

It was time to get back to business. This time it was different for me. I was in an ownership position with my husband, and I was going to be directly involved in the decision-making and company operations. I was scared and a bit nervous but couldn't wait to get started. My husband, the children, and I had a new lease on life.

Fred had been away from the company for almost two years. During the legal battle with his family, we had little or no access to the company's monthly financial statements. When we did finally come to understand the financial situation of the company during the late summer and fall of 1996, the situation was worse than we had anticipated. Sales were way down and staff had been down-sized—the company was basically heading toward receivership. I remember Fred burying his heavy head in his hands, his optimism momentarily gone. "Honey, I don't even know if we can save the company," he said. "I didn't know it was this bad."

WE'RE GOING TO HAVE TO CALL YOUR LINE OF CREDIT

There was no turning back now. We did the only thing we could do: We got to work. We met with our hog producers, our unionized employees, and our customers, sharing our plans for the future and asking for their support. Not too long after reaching the initial settlement terms, we got a most disturbing call from our corporate lender. "Great to have you back, glad you settled that nasty dispute," they said, "but unfortunately, we are serious about calling your line of credit." Guess they saw the books, too!

It never crossed our minds that the bank would pull the plug; we were such optimists that we just assumed everyone shared our enthusiasm and would just let us get down to business. We faced an urgent challenge: find a fast way to raise approximately $33 million in a few weeks for a virtually bankrupt-but-very-high-potential-company, or the bank would close down Intercontinental Packers forever. This would require real stamina and great faith!

How do you find that kind of money? We started with a simple process: creating a list of people or organizations that would benefit if our company prospered. That list included producers, local and far-reaching companies, investment bankers, and individuals. We cast the net wide even including foreign investors half way around the globe, one of whom did come on board.

Then we hit the road. Fred and our financial manager, Steven, flew across the continent; laptops full throttle and cell phones abuzz. They went wherever they felt they had a chance, never looking back as the rejections mounted. They made our case in dozens of meetings. And it was a tough sell—keep in mind one of the country's leading banks had already given their vote of non-confidence in Intercon by pulling our line of credit. There were those who looked at the family feud and

Fred's health problems and assumed the obvious: The company was on its last legs. They sure weren't impressed by me either!

Fortunately, some could look beyond the obvious. Fred and Steven argued that the company still had a base of existing customers and if we even just kept pace with them, we'd grow exponentially. And let's not forget we had Fred Mitchell leading our team a living legend in the industry. And they found some believers. Once we had a few investors committed, others were more willing to listen and the momentum started to build.

FRED IS BACK—WE'RE ON THE ATTACK

Several weeks later, Fred watched with tears of joy welling up in his eyes as two men in dark suits walked up the sidewalk to the front door of our plant the original *Men in Black* with their financial bazookas aimed at our people. The bank didn't think we had the money, and they were ready to close us down. Fred walked up to them with one finger in the air (no, not that finger) and said, "I wouldn't be doing that so quickly if I were you." You see, we had managed to raise the money! It was a tremendous victory for our company. Our dedicated employees gave Fred a standing ovation that day. Endless re-financing negotiations and ongoing efforts to get Fred firmly back running the company were finally paying off. And I'm pleased to say that our wise and daring investors have done very well on what initially appeared to be a risky and some might argue even foolish investment. The slogan "Fred is back we're on the attack" was adopted by some of our people, and an army took to the battlefield.

From the moment we were awarded the pork processing operations, I worked side-by-side with Fred. I had a seat on the board of directors, and Fred and I discussed almost every aspect of the company's operations. He respected my judgment, my intuition, and my insight as a mom shopping and cooking for a family. The whole time, he was patiently teaching me about the business. Fred taught me how to read financial statements, the intricacies of hog supply, and the importance of new product development. We read trade journals together and studied customer contracts. I had no idea how much I would need to rely on this learning.

I'm a big fan of Oprah and what she has accomplished. She is one of the most loving souls on Earth I believe, but on one point, we disagree—that is if she wasn't misquoted. If anyone knows about that, I do! Oprah was once quoted in a top business magazine saying she can't read a balance sheet, but that doesn't matter because she has advisors who worry about this for her. I think this puts her in a potentially precarious position. From my experience, it's absolutely critical that you know your stuff in the business world. As a woman, it helps you win respect. Most importantly, though, this knowledge can protect you from being pegged as a nitwit or a sucker—someone who can be ripped off.

> *It's absolutely critical that you know your stuff in the business world.*

PORK PROCESSOR
KEEPS BOUNCING BACK

Fred and I knew we had to keep moving forward to continue. Our customers were growing and so was their demand. Mega-mergers in the grocery industry meant that customers were looking to us to provide more products. We recognized that if we couldn't meet these demands, our customers would take their whole order and go somewhere else. Fred and I were determined to be aggressive, innovative, and above all, responsive to customer demand.

One of our first steps was re-brand the company. It had been called Intercontinental Packers since Grampa Mendel founded the company in 1940. We felt this was an outdated name that didn't accurately reflect our product. In 1998, we officially changed the company name to Mitchell's Gourmet Foods, reflecting the company's proud family heritage and quality products.

Then we started to look for opportunities to innovate and improve productivity. The meat processing industry is one of the laggards when it comes to automation. In most instances, the work doesn't lend itself to automation; we need the skill and judgment that come from our people. But there are areas where automation can help increase productivity. Fred and I oversaw the development of a robotic arm to separate pork bellies from ribs. When we started discussing the concept of using a robotic arm with our union, we discovered that this particular job is tough on people. This was a task that our hardworking and skilled people did not mind giving up. Our union was behind us all the way. Before long, "Jack the Ribber" was at work alongside our employees. And in fact, the robot's rapid output resulted in the creation of more jobs. Jack the Ribber is the world's first robotic arm used in a commercial pork processing plant and a tremendous success story.

Our hard work was beginning to payoff. We were building a strong customer base across North America, Japan, and the Asian Rim, including large grocery chains such as Safeway, Costco, Loblaws, A&P, and IGA. We were producing their private label pork products, and many were stocking their shelves with Mitchell's brand products as well. Our labor relations were solid, thanks to a strong relationship with our hardworking people. We had contracts in place to secure hog supply—an absolute necessity if we were to continue meeting growing demand. When Fred and I returned to the company, many people questioned whether we could turn around the ailing operation. Our success silenced the naysayers. Once again, there was no question: We had beaten the odds.

FRED MITCHELL WINS TURNAROUND ENTREPRENEUR OF THE YEAR AWARD

By the fall of 1998, people were starting to take notice of our success. Fred was delighted to be named the 1998 Turnaround Entrepreneur of the Year in a national competition. My husband was healthy, our company was recovering, and our family was thriving. We had absolutely no idea that our world was about to fall apart and get sucked into a black hole. The winds of change were beginning to blow.

MY PLAN TO GET ME CLOSER TO MY DREAM:

Get the company running so robustly that no one would dream of coming in and shutting it down.

MY INSTINCTS:

Grow to keep pace with our customers' growth.

THE SEED FOR GOOD:

Employment rises, strong bond forged with our union and suppliers.

Chapter Seven

LIFE LESSON:

Never Give Up on Your Dreams

After Fred's death, it would have been easy for me to cash in my shares of the company and retreat with my children. But that was never my dream. The dream I shared with Fred was to build a robust, thriving company. And it was that vision that I doggedly pursued in those dark days after my return from California.

Many mornings as I woke up, I would keep hoping that this was all a nightmare—that Fred was still alive. When I realized that the nightmare was reality, I forced myself to get out of bed. *Just get up*, I told myself. And then I'd get to work on making our dream a reality. To give up would mean that I had lost everything.

Fred Mitchell dies;
plant officials vow business as usual.

— ***Star Phoenix***, **October 20, 1998**

There are times in your life when a cosmic two-by-four hits you between the eyes. When someone you love with all your heart and soul takes his last breath, you fall to your knees like a bowl full of Jell-O. You wonder how you can possibly go on—or if you even want to.

My world came tumbling down on October 17, 1998. Fred and I had traveled to Stanford Medical Center for a medical check-up. He hadn't had a proper check-up in years; finally, we had the time to make this important trip. His health had been good, and his spirit was strong. We had been the odds beaters for so long now: That's all we knew, that's all we would entertain.

> *There are times in your life when a cosmic two-by-four hits you between the eyes.*

On this particular trip, Fred was having a very simple ultrasound test. Afterward, the nurses told me not to go in to see him quite yet. But I had a strange feeling (intuition) and something in me needed to see him. I went into the hospital room and saw he was in obvious crisis—the heart monitor was going crazy; things were buzzing and beeping. The air was still, but the room was abuzz.

I fell to the floor and screamed as only a wife half-crazed can scream, "God, NO!" I absolutely lost it. I ran into the ladies' room, fell on my face, and threw up all over the room and myself. I lost control—I went crazy pulling my hair and scratching the walls. Finally, after planting my fist through one of them, I dropped to my knees and cried as I have never cried. Tears flowed—all hell had broken loose and I was being whisked away in its fury. For the first time in my life, I was hollow and empty.

When I came out, there was a pastor with a Bible saying, "Let me read to you."

I said, "This isn't real. What's going on—is this some sick joke?" We'd beaten the odds so many times, and this wasn't supposed to be a risky procedure. How could this be happening?

Somehow the indestructible and inspiring spirit I knew in this world as Fred Mitchell survived the night. Our doctor admitted that Fred had baffled him in life and was continuing to do so. I was holding Fred's gentle hand when his breath stopped at 7 o'clock the next morning. I kissed the earthly shell of this precious man, closed my swollen dried out and scratchy eyes, and went to this phenomenal place filled with every species of butterfly and a bright kaleidoscope of colors. Fred always loved butterflies. While I was there in spirit, a big beautiful monarch butterfly landed on my shoulder and fluttered its glorious wings. I got an incredible rush of peace. That was the last peaceful feeling I felt for a very long time. But it was the catalyst for what was to follow.

WHERE'S DADDY?

The hours and days following Fred's death were a complete blur. I made very few, if any, phone calls—only the necessary corporate ones. In my racing mind, I was always cuddled with our children. In my heart and frantic state, I felt compelled to chatter endlessly to Fred— I felt he would hear me!—although so alone now, so empty, and so hollow.

I boarded a plane stunned and robotic—barely alive without a clue. I know now I was in shock. I have no recollection of the long trip home. How would I tell three fragile little children that their daddy wouldn't be coming home ever again? They ran to hug me when I walked through the door. "Where's Daddy?" I broke down— because the children were miles away—mentally. Although we were now together physically, I was completely devastated. How would I ever keep my promises, get my bearings straight—how could I carry on?

I just couldn't believe he died. It wasn't supposed to happen like this. We had been so fortunate, so in love, so blessed. Now I felt cheated and robbed. Desperate for answers, I ran to the bathroom and splashed cold water on my face. Doubts began to creep in, fear reared its ugly head, and anger welled up inside. Why him? Why now? To my left was the spot he used to sit—in his favorite chair— now it was empty and cold. I hated that chair for a moment.

When I stumbled out the door grabbing the wall for support, the children took one look at me and were shocked and bewildered. They were old enough to understand what it meant that their daddy died. My heart broke over and over again as they sobbed in my arms as the reality set in. Three little precious innocent babies. We literally fell on top of each other repeatedly—our knees just gave out. But I knew that I couldn't fall apart, let them down, and take a tumble.

I would provide and protect them no matter what. It wouldn't be like when I was a teenage mom; this time would be different. I wouldn't crack. My children needed me to be strong. Fred would have expected it. I did what I've always done in a time of crisis: find a solution, find a resolve. I asked myself: *What is best here? How can I give it life? How can I move through this space, do what is right?* I prayed and asked for help. Then I got up and kept moving forward.

"I am going to make it," I vowed. My children and I have each other, we will love each other through it, and we will WIN! I thought business could wait a day or two because it wasn't my priority, but it couldn't. It started the morning of Fred's funeral, shoving its face into mine full force. My adversaries assumed the vulnerable young widow would sell Mitchell's and retire rich. After all, the company was now viable—a miracle in its own right. There were those who wrongly assumed the kids and I would ride quietly off into the sunset or even back to California as fast as we could. We had lived happily in Palm Springs, and some thought the children and I might peacefully resume our life there, take the money and run—leave the dream.

I did what I've always done in a time of crisis: find a solution, find a resolve. Come hell or high water, I am here long term.

Let's face it, in business a lot of people don't say, "Well, hey, Fred has this wife. Maybe she's the gal to take on the job of running the business." Especially his "piece of fluff wife" (beauty queen marries business tycoon). God forbid—you'd have to be a complete idiot to say that. Or would you? If anything, those outsiders looking in would think that's a good joke, and the little pretty woman would definitely be the punch line.

My feelings following Fred's death went from rage at him, at myself, at the world and heavens for that matter—to despair—and then to a sudden sense of peace when I remembered that I still had the same stuff inside me that we drew upon to make the original husband and wife business partner blueprint for our dreams. I decided right then and there that come hell or high water, no one would destroy what we were creating. And that meant I wouldn't sell out to the circling vultures who just wanted to scoop up our market share, and I wouldn't be taking the advice of certain executives (fat cats) who could get even richer by brokering my late husband's family heritage to the highest bidder.

In either scenario, I'd have a big bank account. But Mitchell's and the families of committed employees would be toast. They'd rape us for our brand name—private label business and future food service customers—and slam the door in the face of our hardworking and committed people. They would dismantle our dream and our corporate family. We were the largest private employer in the area at that time with a staff of more than 1,000. That made Mitchell's bigger than the population of most small towns in Saskatchewan, like the ones I had grown up in. If I'd let the vultures rule, it would have a devastating impact on our people, our sales force, suppliers, buyers, and customers. It would be a distressing defeat for Fred's good name and memory, the children and me, and I knew at least one angel in the heavens who wouldn't be sleeping. I had to do what a girl has got to do and do it fast: No time to waste.

SHE'S A BUILDER

I've been asked many times why I didn't take the easy route and sell my shares in the company after my husband's death. After all, I was suddenly single parenting three young children. Who needed the stress and corporate intrigue? My answer is that it comes down to a fundamental philosophy that Fred and I shared. This belief is articulated perfectly in a poem titled "Which Am I"—author unknown—about the difference between those who build and those who dismantle:

I watched them tearing a building down
A gang of men in a busy town
With a ho heave to and a hardy-o
They swung a beam and the side wall fell

I asked the foreman, "Are these men skilled,
Like the ones you'd hire if you had to build"
He gave me a laugh and said, "No indeed
Common labor's all I need.
I can easily wreck in a day or two
What builders have taken a year to do."

I thought to myself as I went my way
Which of these roles have I tried to play?
Am I the builder who works with care
Measuring life with a rule and square?
Am I shaping my deeds to a well made plan
Patiently doing the best I can?
Or am I the wrecker who walks the town
Content with the labor of tearing down?
Which am I?
Which are you?

Fred and I had been putting our heart and soul into building the company. While our turnaround had begun, it was still fragile and in need of several crucial elements when Fred died. Just as our planning envisioned, ultimately, the way to secure the company's future was to make it so successful no one would dare shut it down or hurt it. We wanted to ensure closure would simply be a bad business decision. The solution: expand with a state-of-the-art facility. Expansion would provide a valuable business asset long into the future. And expansion would provide the capacity to meet the growing needs of our customers. If the turnaround was to continue, our team had to go for the brass ring. The fundamental equation of our original plan—expand or perish—loomed larger than ever after my husband left this world.

SHE'S DEVELOPED EYES IN THE BACK OF HER HEAD TO KEEP HER COMPANY FROM BEING HIJACKED BY A CORPORATE RAIDER

It certainly didn't take long for the battle for our company to begin. First, behind my back, a Board of Directors meeting was called for the morning of Fred's funeral. I told the instigators that if the meeting proceeded, I'd be there. But I also told them I was preparing my children to attend their father's funeral, and I was not pleased or impressed that the meeting had been called, that it had been called the day of the funeral, and that it had been called without my knowledge. It was sacrilegious and an insult to Fred's good memory. The meeting was canceled; guess they figured it out—DUH!

More than 2,000 people—friends, business executives, community leaders, and many of our family of hard workers—crowded into a church complete with big screens to accommodate the overflow to pay tribute to Fred.

Just minutes after Fred's touching funeral, one of the central players in the corporation told me not to worry about anything; he'd already tracked down a buyer for the company and would solve all my problems. He was positioning himself as a broker—set to make himself a little money on the side—by negotiating a deal to sell the business the same day I buried my husband. Talk about a busy guy!

> Occasionally in business and in life, you come face-to-face with a jackass.

He explained in a most condescending tone that while Fred had been a brilliant businessman, he wasn't a "numbers man." And because Fred didn't understand the numbers, he didn't understand how risky a venture this place is. If my late husband had understood the numbers, the would-be broker told me, Fred would have counseled me to sell the business if he ever died. The loudmouth told me the safest bet was to get out right away rather than oversee the company spiraling into the ground and lose my entire fortune. "That's not what he would have wanted for you and the kids," he assured me with a sweet smirk and a twinkling eye.

Occasionally in business and in life, you come face-to-face with a jackass. I have a technique for dealing with such sticky situations, and I used it with this guy. Rather than seeing the face of the annoying individual, I superimpose the head of a donkey—sort of like the animated donkey Eddie Murphy played in *Shrek*. He kept talking, and I just kept visualizing his donkey head with the fat little animated lips flapping in the wind. "Who invited this jackass to the party," I wondered. He was relieved of his duties shortly thereafter, not as an emotional knee-jerk reaction, but as a sound business decision.

We Don't Like it When Mrs. Mitchell Is Upset

In a matter of days following the funeral, a major creditor got into the act. I was ushered into a formal meeting with the creditor's representatives. When Fred was alive, this creditor apparently considered us a solid bet. Now that Fred was dead, they wanted me to guarantee one of our loans personally. I told them I wouldn't. If they were relating this story, they'd probably tell of some rather direct language and my petite fist making contact with the meeting table on several occasions. It was a standoff.

I knew our shareholders had already closed ranks around me, so I phoned one shareholder group. A representative asked to be put on the speakerphone. He told the creditor: "You've angered Mrs. Mitchell, and we don't like it when Mrs. Mitchell is upset. I suggest you consider." Within an hour, I received a call saying it had all been a misunderstanding, and they really didn't need a personal guarantee. To their credit, this turned out to be a wise investment for them as well as a very wise decision.

We were up against some big, powerful players with deep pockets and big bats. Some shareholders inside the company may have wanted to make a quick buck by selling out, and some competitors would be happy to see our food company disappear. I learned to recognize that people who come across as sincere in one moment might just be out for themselves in the next. I quickly learned to be on guard and never just coast on any front. I'd grown up a girl fending for herself on the wrong side of town and that had taught me about fat cats and blowhards. I had met my fair share of shysters and knew how to both deal with them effectively and avoid ever becoming one of them. I decided if I was going to implement our plan and take hold of the business, I'd better get at it.

> *I learned to recognize that people who come across as sincere in one moment might just be out for themselves in the next.*

LuAn Mitchell Takes Over Family Company

The morning after the funeral, I invited our executive team to our home for coffee in the sunroom. They didn't know what to expect, and I was pretty sure I could see their knees knocking. If I were going to sell my shares, it would spin the company into huge uncertainty. Right off the bat, I told them I had no intention of selling the company. There was an audible sigh of relief. I asked our plant manager, Stu Irvine, a 30-year-plus Mitchell's employee who had started on the packing plant floor, if he'd assume the presidency. Fred and I always felt, although we never discussed it, that Stu was the ideal person to lead the company. He'd worked hard and risen through the ranks. As a result, the union respected him and he understood every aspect of our business. Stu said he'd be honored; I was delighted that he accepted. The next step was to take it to the Board, which approved Stu's appointment. At the same meeting, the Board selected me as Chairperson.

Then I decided to tune out the naysayers and champion the business that Fred and I had fought so hard for and turned around with great passion. I wasn't about to give in to long odds. If Mitchell's was to stay afloat long enough to get the necessary expansion underway, they needed me to stay fully committed and focused. All I had were my shares in the company, and I was determined to retain my majority shareholder position.

> *I was one passionate woman on a mission— someone not to be messed with.*

Some people say I gambled everything on Mitchell's, and I guess that's true. My company shares were all that I owned. If I failed, I was dead in the water and there would be choruses of "I told you so's." But

I didn't view it as a gamble. I wasn't a one-woman show: I had Fred's spirit in the lead, and I had the indomitable Mitchell's team behind me. I was one passionate woman on a mission—someone not to be messed with.

LuAn Mitchell Takes Her Place in Firm's Boardroom

One of the most powerful experiences of my life occurred when I returned to our plant after Fred's death. There was a line of employees, our beautiful Mitchell's family, waiting to greet me with hugs and words of encouragement. I will never forget their warm welcome. I think they recognized that I was from the West side of town (supposedly the "wrong side of the tracks") where the Mitchell's plant was located. How "wrong" could that be when nestled here were all these beautiful people and great works? Once people get to know me, they recognize that there's nothing hoity-toity about me. A socialite I'm not: I love a little glitter now and then, but my feet are firmly planted on solid ground. The warm and supportive response I got from our employees only made me more determined to find a thousand ways if necessary to get the company in so strong a position and healthy that no one would ever dare consider shutting it down. We were on a roll.

Then one morning my phone rang in the office. "LuAn?" an inquiring voice asked.

"Yes," I answered puzzled.

"This is 'so and so' from 'blah blah news.'"

"Oh, yea. What can I do for you?" I asked.

"Well, we heard you never invited your in-laws to your husband's funeral. Why not?"

"Just great," I responded in frustration. "I wasn't throwing a party and assembling a guest list. I arranged my husband's funeral exactly according to his wishes. That is what I did—like it or lump it, fella. Good-bye." My day was set into a tailspin—when will all this finally vaporize and just go away? I decided that would be up to me and I put it away right then and there. I forgave them all, including the guy who called me, and I took the high road back to work!

Chairing my first Board meeting was an intimidating experience. But I felt Fred's presence at my side. Wear navy blue if you mean business, he always said, so I wore a dark blue pantsuit. I knew that it was important to have a smooth transition to the new executive team because we were poised to launch an Initial Public Offering ("IPO") and take the company public. We wanted a strong launch on the stock market, and we had to minimize any disruptions at the executive level.

Although I had sat in on several Board meetings as a director and was familiar with the protocol, I had never chaired a meeting. I started with a moment's silence for Fred. Then we got down to business. I masked my initial fears with a brash exterior that day. I might have been a bit overbearing, but I didn't care because I'd just been through quite enough hell. And I was the majority shareholder now, I knew that I had the power. I wanted people to know they weren't dealing with a weak, weeping widow here. My objectives were clear: We were going to make the place big enough and powerful enough that someone would have to be crazy to try to shut it down. I didn't know how I was going to do it right.

I tuned them out—but never numbed myself out. Be careful: There is a difference.

But I was determined to do it. My family's nest egg was invested in the future of this great company.

Many, many people thought I was going to lose it all. I couldn't even consider that possibility. "The girl's an idiot," I heard some say.

"Fred would roll over in his grave if she tries to carry this out. She's going to lose everything he worked so hard to build." I tuned them out—but never numbed myself out. Be careful: There is a difference.

In my new position as Chair of the company, I wanted to show our new executive team where I was coming from. I gave an audiotape *The Greatest Salesman in the World* as a gift to our new President, Stu Irvine, and our Vice President of Sales, Mike Burke. I found this tape hugely helpful and inspiring and knew it would help Stu and Mike understand my mindset and where my heart was in business and otherwise. To their credit, they accepted the gift with enthusiasm. This gave me confidence that we had chosen our new team well. One must be open-minded and not take offense at times like these. Remember: Never look a gift-horse in the mouth.

FRED MITCHELL MEMORIAL SCHOLARSHIP PROGRAM LAUNCHED

When I was faced with the painful, traumatizing task of writing Fred's obituary, I had to decide where in memoriam donations should be directed. This was a tough choice: There were so many worthy causes that Fred would want to support. But when I thought about what was really dear to Fred's heart, I thought about helping young people, the ones who fall in the cracks, the less fortunate souls. And I came up with the idea of somehow helping youth at risk. We created the Fred Mitchell Memorial Scholarship Program, a fund that provides scholarships to help youth at risk get off the street and continue their education. The reaction from friends, business leaders, and community members was positive, and donations were generous. Together, we planted a wonderful seed for good.

The Fred Mitchell Scholarship Program helps beautiful, intelligent but yet challenged young people to grow and be all that they can be. It reflects Fred's philosophy of changing the world into a better, kinder place one heart at a time. Our stipulation is that scholarship recipients have taken the necessary steps to deal with any addictions and get off the streets. Each year, we get clothing and beauty salon services donated as a special treat for the scholarship recipients. I meet with them and take them out for a meal; I love to spend time together.

At one dinner, the scholarship recipient was covered in brazen tattoos. She was nervous about taking off her beaten-up leather coat and exposing the tattoos. I told her that if you are comfortable in your skin, the aesthetics of the outer shouldn't be a hindrance. In other words, you're perfect and complete just the way you are, and hey, you WON! Now you've got another chance—you can do something about it if you wish. She moved me deeply when she proudly removed her coat and sat straight as an arrow by my side. I made it a point to see the beautiful girl within. She was just barely living in a tiny room at the YWCA, and this little lost child maintained a 77% average in her studies after winning the scholarship. I am told she has now become a social worker to help others. She could have been bitter and given up. But instead, she blossomed.

> *If you are comfortable in your skin, then you're perfect and complete just the way you are.*

It has been especially gratifying to me to provide support for young single moms who want to further their education. One of our scholarship recipients has gone on to become a mentor for youth at risk and married a great guy who loves her and her young son.

We recently awarded a scholarship at the Academy for Business Leadership in Los Angeles, an inspiring non-profit organization that provides underserved youth with opportunities to learn at college campuses. It was especially gratifying to go back to Fred's hometown and provide a *hand up* to another beautiful young person. We continue to plant seeds for good. I can think of no greater tribute to Fred's memory. These beautiful young people also receive a guardian angel named "Fred" as part of the deal. How good is that? They serve as great mentors to many others and me.

I WILL ALWAYS RUN TO YOU WHEN YOU NEED ME

In those early weeks and months following Fred's death, I felt his presence close to me. I scolded to him many times, saying, "Don't even think that you're going anywhere because I need your help." And I did need his help; it was part of my healing. I put on a tough "chick who can take it" look for the outside world and a strong "Mom's okay; we'll be just fine" face for my children. But I was often lonely, shaky, scared, and extremely sad. I hardly slept for the first four months. And I desperately wanted to: I believed Fred would send me messages in my dreams. I thought he would use that means to give me a sign—I just felt it. But every night I went to bed with my head spinning. Sleep was elusive and I was looking the part with my baggy eyes and pale skin.

One night when I finally slept from sheer exhaustion, I dreamt about being outside an apartment building. I saw some rough looking juvenile delinquents who scared me. When I saw the building manager inside, I tried to wave him over to let me into my apartment—I couldn't find my key. Suddenly the punks ran right past me and went after the manager. I ran around to the back of the building, collapsing, and finally resting on a bench. I looked over and saw a shadowy man come from behind the building. When he came closer, I saw it was Fred. He started walking toward me, and then he started running. He sat on the bench beside me and said, "Honey, did you see that?" It was amazing because in real life, he couldn't run due to a herniated disk in his back and several other problems. "I can do anything now. We can do anything," Fred told me. "I will always run to you when you need me. Don't be afraid when you think someone is going to come in and take our people because you'll know what to do." Then he was gone.

When I woke up from that dream, I felt peaceful and confident. I had no doubt that my guardian angel was by my side. From that night on, I slept like a baby. I was so satisfied and content that I may have even purred!

MITCHELL'S TO LAUNCH IPO

We knew we had to make changes at many levels of operation in order to keep up with massive consolidation in the grocery industry and yet gain entry into the food service sector. The path laid out in the plan we constructed was to pursue major expansion and modernization of our operations. We planned to pay the millions of dollars our expansion would cost by issuing an IPO and become listed on the stock market. In fact, Fred's death happened just weeks before we were set to take the company public, putting me in a most precarious position.

The homework was all done. The binders of information on taking Mitchell's public would have sunk the Titanic without need of an iceberg. Immediately after Fred's death, I immersed myself totally in the idea of going public—no different from before his passing. One of my jobs was to assemble a killer Board of Directors, something we had not done yet. Running a public company was like sailing in uncharted waters for our team and for me, and I wanted the best help available.

The top of the corporate mountain in our hometown of Saskatoon is an international company known as the Potash Corporation
of Saskatchewan ("PCS"). It's the largest potash producer on the
face of the earth and a multi-billion dollar entity. I wanted the
highly respected head of PCS—Chair and President Chuck
Childers—to sit on the Board of our publicly traded company.
Chuck's a busy man, and appointments to see him are hard to come
by. But I didn't have time to wait. One day, I just planted myself in
his office, toting luggage filled with IPO binders. I suspect by the
looks I was getting that his secretary would have preferred that I got
lost. But I didn't. To his everlasting credit, Chuck eventually saw me.

At first, I hit a brick wall. He explained that he spent much of
his time traveling around the world and serving on our board wasn't
in the cards. But my gut told to me keep talking, so I went for it.
The more we talked, the more he opened up. He empathized with
my situation—Fred had just died, and there was no choice but to
expand the company, or it would die, too. I pleaded with him and
like few others, he understood and agreed that the way to fund
expansion was going public. Chuck began to wonder if he had been
in Fred's unfortunate position if there would be people willing to assist
his widow in such a grand adventure as taking a family business
public—and only days after the funeral. I think he talked himself into
agreeing to serve on the Mitchell's Board. Too bad I'd never get the
chance to take him up on his generous offer!

MITCHELL'S SHELVES PLANS
TO GO PUBLIC

Launching a successful IPO is a tempting and very seductive propo-
sition. I've never been wined and dined so much in my life. And let's
face it: I stood to make a lot of money if Mitchell's went public. So

would several of our other shareholders. That's why some of them were so upset when I called off the IPO. "That woman is nuts," I could hear them say.

There's a certain prestige to being a public company, but there are a lot of advantages to staying private, too. Going public had seemed like a no-brainer to Fred and me—an obvious way of raising the money we needed to take the company to the next logical stage of its growth and launch it into the big leagues. But I realized that going public now would also leave Mitchell's vulnerable to a hostile takeover. And even though there were precautions we could take to fend off a takeover, in the aftermath of Fred's death, the vultures would be more aggressive.

If there had been any minor worries when Fred was around, they would take no prisoners when only Fred's sweet little widow was at the helm. I had no intention of letting them try. As we started exploring our options, my gut began aching, telling me that we needed to rethink this strategy. My gut went on to tell me to stop the public offering in its tracks even though in many ways this made no sense at all. I had assembled an awesome Board of Directors and our people were revved up now—only days before we were set to announce it. I wasn't sure; it was a huge business decision and even though my instinct said it was the right move, it took a great deal of daring to deviate from the initial plan that had served us so well.

Introspection Develops Instincts

What if you feel you don't have strong instincts or rarely feel gut reactions, second-guessing yourself more often than not? It could be because you've been suppressing your instincts, numbing out. To give your inner knowledge a voice, you need to make time for peaceful introspection. Sure, we need to look to external sources and mentors for information. But once you've done your homework—read the industry news, consulted trusted advisors, surveyed the market-place—it's time to trust what you know internally, even root it out. I heard a great speaker once who said if you over "anal-ize" everything, you'll always get a crappy outlook. How true!

I think everyone should have a sacred sanctuary. It might be a special corner of your garden, a special comfy chair in a quiet cor-ner, or a home office. My sanctuary is a bathroom. Oh, yeah. You read right. I've got it "all in the can!" It has more art on the walls than in my entire first home. It's decorated with my favorite colors and fabrics. There are gold but-terflies on the ceiling and candles everywhere and a custom-ordered Kohler tub that has back massage jets and foot massage jets. The sales-woman I ordered it through cautioned that I shouldn't buy it because it was very expensive and well, I really am not tall enough; I am five feet and four inches tall. I told her not to worry—I would wear my high heels!

> *To give your inner knowledge a voice, you need to make time for peaceful introspection.*

The goofy thing is the tub is shaped for girls like me in its curves. I fit just fine! She obviously didn't do her homework. Perhaps the best design feature of my special place is a lock on the door that ensures my privacy. Almost everyday, I soak in a delightful bubble bath in my very own dream tub and enjoy solitary thinking time with a fra-grant bath bomb, candles, and a big bottle of Perrier. If you think this sounds selfish, you're missing the point. This 10 or 15 minutes to myself is an investment that pays off handsomely. I tell my fam-ily it's my time-out, and they respect that. I'm a better wife, parent, a more thoughtful friend to myself and others, and a more effective leader. Not to forget that I am cleaner for it, and I smell good, too!

And I have personal instincts that I trust implicitly. They tell me to take a little "time away" now and then—and I listen. My family loves me enough and knows me well enough to say, "Mom, why don't you take a bath," when they see I'm worked up. I don't do drugs. This is so much better all around!

A Woman Boss in the Macho World of Meatpacking

It didn't take me long to relax and start enjoying my role as Chair of Mitchell's. But I realized that I needed to do some homework if I wanted to succeed in such a male-dominated environment. I turned to books to find out how my mentors could help me. I read about "male bonding," about how men process problems, and how they approach various situations. By recognizing how a man's take on a workplace issue may be different from mine, I can understand where they are coming from rather than be frustrated—even infuriated at times—by the difference. That applies to all of us. Guys and gals can get it together better if we try to understand each other a bit better.

I was also reminded that a little humor can go a long way in developing business relationships. On my first business trip with my executive team after Fred's death, we were rushing for a plane hoping to sit in the lounge a moment before our flight. I set off that nasty buzzing noise going through the airport security metal detector. My colleagues—all of them men—stopped in their tracks to see what the problem was. The airport security officer (a burly woman who looked like Olga from Russia) continued to wave her noisy wand back and forth frantically across my chest. It was the underwire in my new French lace bra (even meatpackers have some nice undies). She finally figured it out and loudly announced, "Oh, it's your bra!" I shrugged and said to them: "Get used to it, guys!" And off we went. (I'm pretty sure I heard someone make a reference to the boss wearing a steel-studded bra, but that's okay!)

The decision not to go public was a tough one. Some shareholders were extremely opposed to my decision. Let's face it: We might have all walked away with a great deal of money. This was the first time that I had thrown my weight around—all 110 pounds of me—as majority shareholder, and some people weren't happy about it. I could sense them thinking, *It's okay if this blonde, ambitious piece of fluff is going to be here. But now she's getting pushy.* But I wasn't about to start listening to the naysayers now. I was too busy looking for a solution to our prob-

> *By recognizing how a man's take on a workplace issue may be different from mine, I can understand where they are coming from.*

lems. We still desperately needed to expand our business, and we didn't have much time to do it—it had to be right the first time. We didn't have the money to pay for expansion and couldn't take on more debt. We had to shift gears quickly from devoting all our energy to the IPO to searching for new alternatives. But I had a calm faith that we were heading in the right direction.

MY PLAN TO GET ME CLOSER TO MY DREAM:

Keep the company healthy, growing, and in Saskatoon.

MY INSTINCTS:

Don't sell.

THE SEED FOR GOOD:

The tremendous love and support I receive from my children, family, friends, and people at Mitchell's.

Chapter Eight

LIFE LESSON:

No Dream Is Achieved Alone

No matter what your goal, you probably can't get there on your own. Even elite athletes involved in solitary sports need the support of their coach, their family, and their sponsors. Who's on your team? Have you assembled one yet? If you have a clear, compelling goal that you believe in passionately, you are definitely able to attract believers and supporters to your team while holding true to yourself.

If you told a so-called friend that you would have a million dollars in five years, would they laugh at you, or would they say, "Great, how can I help?" It's important to share your dream passionately with the people around you.

*Widow's true grit
saves family business.*

— *Possibility Thinkers Digest*, **August 2001**

*E*ntering 1999, the survival of Mitchell's Gourmet Foods was on the line. I instinctively knew we needed to form some kind of partnership or alliance. I wasn't sure who it would be or when it would happen, but I had to be sure this relationship would be in keeping with our objectives. I decided, very uncharacteristically of me, to personally attend a meeting with a competitor to discuss supply issues. Now I was faced with another really tough decision.

I've always believed it's essential to have trusted and loyal people around on whom you can rely.

A big part of our success at Mitchell's has always been our people. They're noble and hardworking—the best really—and walking with them has made a difficult road smoother more than once. I've always believed it's essential to have trusted and loyal people around on whom you can rely. When our new company President Stu Irvine came to me with the suggestion, I listened. Even though he knew I'd resist the idea, Stu raised the possibility of talking to Schneider Foods. Schneiders is one of Canada's largest producers of premium-processed meat, fresh pork, poultry, and grocery products. They have about 12 manufacturing facilities across Canada and are owned by the large American hog producer, Smithfield Foods, out of Virginia. Schneiders is the only competitor I would have considered talking to in this trusted way.

There were compelling synergies: They were the biggest in Eastern Canada, and we were the biggest in Western Canada. Both Mitchell's and Schneiders are long-term family businesses; both have the same high level of quality and integrity in both product and staffing relations. And there had already been some connection between the two companies. My husband late Fred and Douglas Dodds, President of Schneiders, had served together on the Canadian Meat Council. And though I didn't know it at the time, Mitchell's founder, Fred Mendel, and Schneider's founder, Fred Schneider, had talked about bringing their businesses together back in the 1970s.

In the world of the late 1990s, Mitchell's and Schneiders also had common problems: We were both struggling to secure an adequate supply of hogs, and we were both going to have to contend with a brazen and aggressive competitor opening a huge new plant that could further erode our supply. There were inquiries from many others, but I felt that Schneiders was a fit; my gut told me so.

MITCHELL'S, SCHNEIDERS JOIN FORCES

Stu initiated a meeting, and I went in with an open mind. That was the first of many meetings over the coming weeks. We brought in our lawyers and started to negotiate in the direction of a strategic partnership. It was complicated, and it was arduous. But throughout the process, I had my eye on our goal. My objectives with this alliance, as always, were simple: to be able to keep our company growing and not sell anyone or anything out. We spent long grueling days and nights hammering out a palatable agreement, and we finally had a deal. It was a good one for both companies' futures. Schneiders acquired a 32% interest in Mitchell's. In return, we got the cash we needed to fund our much-needed expansion.

Our corporate strategic alliance with Schneiders made us both stronger while remaining autonomous. Both companies continued to operate with complete autonomy, ensuring that we maintained our individual strengths, and we now had the necessary resources to build our future on firm ground.

Mitchell's now had the ability and momentum to expand without risk of exposing ourselves to a hostile corporate public company takeover. In April 1999, we publicly announced the strategic alliance with Schneider and an expansion: a $44 million project that would double our capacity in a core sector of our business and increase our workforce by more than 200 people right off the top, with more to follow. As a result of the investment, by 2001, Mitchell's employed more than 1,600 people—the highest in our history. It was a proud day. This is one powerful partnership and probably the best move our company has ever made. In 2002, the alliance progressed to the next practical and logical step with Schneiders acquiring my stake in Mitchell's.

No Dream Is Achieved Alone

When Fred and I took over the company in 1996, one of our first moves was to talk to our union. Fred met with the union leaders, and he spoke to our entire workforce as a group. I stood by his side— literally. He was honest about the challenges we faced and our commitment to doing whatever it would take in building the company.

As a result, the union was receptive, willing, and able to work with us to achieve our goals. We had put it all on the line and people knew it. Even though headlines had accused us of living "high off the hog," that was far from the truth. We had a small rental home in Saskatchewan and our Palm Springs house—no private jets, servants, or yachts. That is how nutty things can get in the headlines. But now it was "put up or shut up." We were going to sink or swim together.

Don't become numb to the world around you and all it offers. Quite often, the help you need is there for the taking.

I've had some fabulous teachers and mentors on my team for years. Sometimes, I didn't recognize them; sometimes, I did. I'm a voracious reader on a wide range of subject matters—from how animals function—to grammar and vocabulary—and always anything on positive thinking. When I face a challenge or a new situation, I often find the support I need in a great book or audiotape. I always work hard to soak up the wealth of information that's around us and decipher it later if need be. Don't become numb to the world around you and all it offers. Quite often, the help you need is there for the taking.

Magnificent Mentors

Fred Mitchell was my mentor, just as Fred Mendel was his. What an opportunity to learn from someone who knows a business inside out. Fred had worked firsthand at many jobs in our plant so he could see issues from many points of view. He understood and respected our people; he was one of them and never created an hierarchy, and they returned the affection and admiration. One of the most powerful learning experiences of my life was having my husband and mentor patiently and lovingly teach me about our company and his philosophies. I watched and listened and then I grew into a new person.

If you feel you don't have a mentor, find one . . . or several! I believe that part of human nature is that we all like to help people even if it's hidden deep down at the time. If you appear as someone who will truly benefit from someone giving you his or her time and knowledge, he or she may generously offer it.

Look for a shining star in your same line of business or the one you wish to enter. Find a great person doing things that you admire who has enough experience and patience that they can teach you something. And don't forget that other element of human nature. In any relationship, people are wondering what's in it for them. To see you grow and blossom, and feel they were a part of that is a wonderful feeling. They may even become a future investor with cash and not just time. Never underestimate the "power of planting" those seeds for good you plant along the way. This can amaze you repeatedly. Ah, the sweet smell of success—that fragrant garden you will grow will bless you forever.

A mentor has the opportunity to educate, influence, and feel the immense satisfaction of helping someone succeed. All the senses are stimulated and invigorated. Show your appreciation for people who help you in your quest. Thank you notes, handwritten or commercial, or even a quick e-mail are an appropriate way of demonstrating your bloom. And don't ever forget to give back; someone may be looking to you as a mentor or need your time or sharing. You might be surprised at how much you learn by mentoring someone and how much you are ahead in the game already. And I guarantee the experience will be tremendously satisfying for you. Maybe you'll prevent someone from being taken advantage of or from falling when they could have skated past an obstacle. Be open to these opportunities to plant a seed of good, nurture it, watch it grow, and never under-estimate your role. Grow, but always give back.

INTRODUCE THEM TO LUAN!

I have developed pretty accurate instincts about people. My lawyers joke that if they want the goods on someone, they say, "Introduce them to LuAn." I can generally sense pretty quickly if they are a person of integrity. Although I don't judge people, the sifting process goes on.

Show your appreciation for people who help you in your quest.

There is a story about a snake. It seems a large, kind-hearted snake took up residence in front of a school over the summer holidays. Although he looked intimidating, he was not mean at all. He would never bite anyone. In the fall when the children returned, some of the boys dared each other to kick the big ugly snake. They were scared. But finally, the class bully took the first shot. Then when the snake did not react, others followed beating the snake within an inch of its life. The school bell rang, and the children ran off laughing.

In order to see through others, you must be willing to let others see through you; you get what you give, and it starts with integrity.

A wise old man who had seen the whole thing from the park across the street came over to the snake that was barely alive. The snake asked, "Why did they do this? I did not do any-thing—I love the children." The old man answered the snake: "Just because you don't bite doesn't mean you can't hiss!"

Now and then, my friend, we all will need to hiss.

Often, appearances mean nothing—always look beyond, and be wise! In order to see through others, you must be willing to let others see through you; you get what you give, and it starts with integrity. I use my instincts to evaluate the people I'm working with and if a warning bell goes off in my head, no matter how good someone looks on the outside, I listen to that warning. I call them "red flags." I figure these people are possibly better suited somewhere else. I see them receiving their highest good—wherever that may lead. I bless them silently and let them go—never looking back. If it is meant to be, we will meet again and go from there.

> *Often, appearances mean nothing— always look beyond, and be wise!*

Looking for the Kind Eyes

I'm a careful observer of people—not a judge, an observer. There is a huge difference. Ever since I was a child, I've watched for people with kind eyes. We had a dear milkman who came to our house when I was a kid, a hardworking, and jovial guy. When he smiled, I noticed his kind eyes. He always bought lemonade from my lemonade stand. He generally even tipped, which to a kid like me, left quite an impression. "Something for nothing"—WOW. I would say, "But sir, that's too much." He would jump back into his milk truck and with a wave he would say, "Good job, LuAn. Keep the change."

I started to think. I liked to walk along the railroad tracks after school looking for the prettiest stones. I found colorful and smooth stones. I gathered them up and wrapped them in a paper towel with a nice ribbon. The next day when the milkman bought my lemonade, I proudly handed him the bundle of wrapped stones. "Thanks, Mr. Milkman." I said, "Keep the present."

Sometimes, I'll see people just walking down the street and when they smile or nod—a kind smile or a gentle nod, I get a rush of peace. It's important to be able to recognize this quality in people. With all the sadness and hurt in the world, we need to stay focused on good people and good deeds. I strive to be one of those people with kind eyes and gentle nods.

I'm a careful observer of people—not a judge, an observer.

In business settings, I also watch people's facial expressions and their body language. Don't get me wrong. I am far from perfect. I can be pretty cautious; I don't need to be everybody's friend. This is not a popularity contest or a pageant. My attitude is show me, don't tell me. Get out there and demonstrate that you believe in your words. And when a red flag goes up, I don't ignore it. Those who would say, "Do as I say, not as I do" are lost. I don't keep people in the circle who don't fit in. I silently release them with love, then out loud with kindness if need be. I always try to imagine them happy and in their right place in my mind. Releasing with love is a great liberator!

IF MY DOG LIKES THEM, THEY'RE IN

After giving a speech recently, I was asked how I know when someone is to be trusted. "If my dog likes them," I answered, "They're in. I think that court cases could be solved sometimes by bringing in the person's dog. If the dog attacks, then you probably found your culprit!" And I wasn't joking! In fact, the Schneider deal was kind of sealed by Babykins.

After our first joint meeting, I invited some of the Schneider executives and our executive team to our acreage for a social drink, a group comprised entirely of businessmen and "little ole" me. When I was off in the kitchen arranging drinks and snacks on a tray, I noticed there was very little noise coming from the living room where the guys were. *Strange*, I thought, *I hope that there are no issues that have developed—better hurry up.* When I walked out, I saw all these tight-lipped very uncomfortable, but classy executives sitting silently, politely staring into space trying not to watch as Babykins entertained them in the middle of the room getting enthusiastically intimate with my little girl's stuffed Winnie the Pooh.

> With all the sadness and hurt in the world, we need to stay focused on good people and good deeds.

Once I got over the embarrassment, kicking her gently with my foot as I balanced the tray and began serving the guests, I realized that Babykins must have liked these people—otherwise, she would never have done this in front of them! She found them to be trustworthy. (Fortunately, I don't have fire poles in my house. If Babykins' mood shifted, we may have had an alarm go off!)

THEY ARE HUMANS FIRST, EMPLOYEES SECOND

The meatpacking industry isn't known for especially healthy union/management relationships. But I'm proud to say that in over 60 years of operation, our company had not had a single strike. This is due in large part to the attitude of our honorable founder, Fred Mendel. He always said the people who work for him are human beings first and employees second. My late husband Fred and I carried forward this philosophy when we became the owners.

When our company was on the ropes in 1996, our union worked cooperatively with us. This harmony reassured investors and helped us edge away from the brink of bankruptcy. Similarly, after Fred's death, when I unexpectedly took over as Chair, the union decided to stick with me. Any nervousness by the union could have caused investors to bolt and made our security impossible. Instead, we stuck together and moved forward together.

I feel a true sense of partnership and pride with our employees. Some of our best ideas and cost-saving measures have come from our unionized workforce. We've worked hard to create a culture where our people are encouraged to tell us if there's a better way to do things. That means they must be confident that their observations, criticisms, and suggestions will be received constructively.

> We would always try to look at new ideas and new approaches as opportunities, not threats.

In many companies and with many managers, employees aren't encouraged to speak up. Yet they are the ones on the frontlines who often know best how to do things better. Fred used to say, "People can find a hundred ways to help you or a hundred ways to screw you." We wanted to play fair and help each other. We would always try to look at new ideas and new approaches as opportunities, not threats.

When we first started exploring the use of robotics in our plant, we discussed the idea with our people, designers, union, and government. Together, we came up with an excellent plan that improved working conditions and created employment. This strong alliance shows that if you have the same goals and faith in those goals, you can overcome anything.

It gets my dander up when people pronounce that there's no such thing as company loyalty anymore. I say these people need to go look in the mirror and ask themselves why not. Have more faith in your people. Mostly, they just want their issues recognized. News Flash! We have loyalty. You can, too. The Mitchell's employees whose parents and grandparents also worked for us are our pride and joy.

Don't talk about the end of company loyalty to the people who proudly accept long service awards. And don't tell that to a fine gentleman like Herman Neumann, Mitchell's oldest living retiree whose 95th birthday party was wall-to-wall with family and friends who love him, including my husband, me, and our son Freddie, who thinks of

> *That's where loyalty comes from—acts like these, putting our hand out to each other to lift and not pull down.*

Herman as a dear grandfather. The historic roots go back a long way. I have seen a heart-wrenching letter written in 1942 by Fred Mendel to a refugee camp in Quebec offering to hire a young Herman Neumann and sponsor him in moving to Saskatoon. In fact, Fred Mendel sponsored dozens of refugees to come work for him during World War II. That's where loyalty comes from—acts like these, putting our hand out to each other to lift and not pull down.

MITCHELL'S BREAKS NEW GROUND WITH PEER SUPPORT PROGRAM

When I was at Mitchell's, we supported its employees in many ways, including the industry's first Peer Support program. Throughout our operations, there are dozens of people with a small butterfly on their helmet. This indicates that they are part of the innovative Peer Support Team. These employees help fellow employees with problems such as substance abuse, family problems, financial challenges, problem teens, and depression. The unique aspect of this program is that people are helped by their peers.

Most of our employees are men, and they can find it difficult to ask for help. Going to a counselor or psychologist's office would be one of the guys' worst nightmares, especially if someone saw you do it! The Peer Support personnel (our volunteer employees) are trained to recognize various symptoms and problems and assist their co-workers through listening, understanding, and providing appropriate referrals when necessary—confidentially. They often meet at the home of the person with the perceived problem. This often increases the comfort factor by allowing the person to be on his or her own turf.

In the first two years of the program, Peer Support personnel had more than 1,300 contacts and helped hundreds of co-workers overcome a wide range of personal issues. The value of this program was driven home one day when we averted a potentially disastrous situation. One of our workers had been on medical leave for several months due to a tragic brain injury. This is a person who had no other family—his job at Mitchell's and his corporate family meant everything to him.

One day, he walked into our plant and told our chief steward matter-of-factly: "If I don't get my job back, I'm going to kill myself." The chief steward knew what to do. He called in our social worker, Mike Dunphy, kicked the plant manager out of his office, and sat down with this troubled and desperate man. Before long, they had taken the deadly knives out of his backpack (he was quite serious about hurting himself and ending his life). After a few meetings with his doctor and a psychiatrist, they came up with a viable solution—a way this man could return to work. Today, he's back working full-time, a highly productive member of our team. Another win-win for all!

When I was there, we felt that as food processors, we have a special responsibility to run a safe, high quality operation. "These aren't widgets we're producing," I would tell everyone. "It's food that people eat." And all of our products have our name on them and Fred

Mitchell's signature, not to mention a "money back" guarantee! We want to know that each person who comes in to work is ready to create a gourmet food product with pride. When I buy a product off the supermarket shelf for my family, I wonder for a moment who made that product. I wonder how they are treated in their workplace and whether they take pride in their products, the way our employees do at Mitchell's. I know the product I'm buying is only as good or as safe as the people who made it.

> *Taking care of our people is both the right thing to do and good business.*

Taking care of our people is both the right thing to do and good business. They feed their families, too, and the high standards they operate under are reflected in their superior work and therefore a first-rate product. Grocery shopping with my kids has always been an awesome experience for me, as we discuss these topics. After we return home, the kids often visit corporate Websites and research corporate conditions and philosophies. That makes me very proud, I must say!

MERRY CHRISTMAS FROM THE MITCHELLS

Our first Christmas after Fred's death was looking like a very sad occasion. The children and I couldn't bear the thought of celebrating Christmas without him. But then I thought about a gem of wisdom I had learned from one of my self-help books. It said that one of the best ways to solve our own problems is to help someone else who's in an even tougher position than we are. Helping others always helps to lighten your own burden and gives you the joy and fulfillment of giving unselfishly.

As that scary Christmas approached, I thought about families who do without at Christmas time. And the children and I started a cherished family tradition. We ask the Mitchell's social worker for a referral to a hurting family who was going through difficult financial times. Just before December 25th, the children and I bring them Christmas.

> One of the best ways to solve our own problems is to help someone else who's in an even tougher position than we are.

We bring a beautiful Christmas dinner, along with table linens, dishes, roasting pot, serving dishes, cutlery, and candles. We also bring gifts for the whole family. Then we leave everything with them, set their table, serve them if they would like, and the children play together as our special Christmas gift. And we receive a great gift back: We deliver our Christmas dinner and gifts as a family, which brings so much more meaning than writing a check or putting food in a drop box.

We have great memories—of the year our vehicle got stuck in a big snow bank because Mommy took a wrong turn and friendly neighbors pushed us out. And memories of my new husband, a bestselling children's book author, reading to two sweet boys as I set the table. God is good! How great this life can be! What a lovely holiday season we shared. These families are mentors, too. Our Christmas "gift" is just one way that we give back. And in giving, we receive so much in return.

BEAUTY QUEEN MEATPACKER MEANS BUSINESS

People don't look at me and say, "Hey, now there's a meatpacker!" And that's an important lesson: Don't judge by appearances. Just because I'm a petite woman who likes to wear feminine and fancy clothes and high heels, don't think I'm a pushover! I also can pop on my work boots and smock with the best of them. I've learned that in business and in life, women face certain obstacles. It's important to recognize those obstacles so you know how to overcome them.

In the early 1990s when Fred was recovering from his transplant and we were living in Palm Springs, I volunteered for an environmental group called "Kids for Saving the Earth." Part of my role was to develop "green" ideas with children. One such idea was a Barbie Earth Summit. Since Barbie dolls are not biodegradable, children would come together to trade Barbies. I actually met with the Environmental Task Force at Mattel, the company that makes and sells Barbies. I presented my case (it didn't go anywhere but hey, you have to try!) and left the meeting. One of the executives accompanied me to the elevator. "You know," he said, looking me up and down. "*You* could be Barbie!" I was seething. *Did you hear a word that I said,* I wondered. I was so discouraged that the lasting impression I might have left at this meeting was my appearance.

I think I've surprised some people with how tough I can be. I'll never forget the first time I had to read my first rendering contract. BARF! BARF! TRIPLE BARF! Rendering is the process of using the remaining parts of slaughtered animals after the meat has been taken. There I was, at a table of numbed-out-dollars-and-cents macho men who had been reading and negotiating these contracts for years. By necessity, these contracts go into detail—fairly grotesque detail I might add—about the disposal of internal organs, skulls, and bones.

When I started reading, I almost vomited. After all, I was the girl who couldn't sit through horror movies as a teenager. I had my eyes closed for almost all of *The Texas Chainsaw Massacre.* And there I was discussing hog bowels. But I put on my tough "go ahead and make my day" face, negotiated the details of the contract, and got on with business. As the saying goes, never let them see you sweat. It would have been seen as a great weakness if I let the rendering details turn my stomach, and I would have let the entire team down. The numbers do matter in business and that's what I focused on—this meatpacking mama wasn't going to crack and drop the ball. I didn't have the freedom to grimace, roll my eyes, or make a face.

As the saying goes, never let them see you sweat.

Later on I thought, *Holy moly, I've really come a long way from the gentle and sweet beauty industry! You look "mahvelous dahling"!* A couple of temper tantrums later that evening in the privacy of my own home, then a long bubble bath, a nice glass of merlot, and a few lit candles flickering can do wonders for a girl like me on a mission. (Some secrets are worth sharing—can we talk?)

Go Ahead—Bring Your Work Home

My new role at Mitchell's was hugely demanding. It was a big change for my children to have a full-time—and then some—working mom, especially as they were also coping with the death and loss of their father. But from the very beginning, I included my children in my working life. I used to believe that we should leave our work at the office. Separate the two no matter what it takes to do it. Then I saw my dedicated but totally exhausted husband struggle to run a business that way. We never talked about anything, and he was always burnt out. That was a taboo between him and his family when they were the owners and players—work here, his wife, children and family there, but like oil and water, never mix it together—at the expense of family unity, his sanity, losing out on moments never recovered (first steps), and ultimately his marriage. His mind was always split even when he was at home—and at work, he became split and fragmented again! He was stressed about it but carried the burden alone.

That's when I got more involved with him and the business—at his invitation. As with most things in life, I jumped in with both feet. We began working as a team—I loved him and therefore I wanted to help him with his load. Fred soon recognized what I could bring to the partnership. I was the ideal consumer: I love cooking, and I love grocery shopping. I'm the Mitchell's customer. I was the grocery shopper in the house. He only frequented the meat counter, whereas I did it all! Fred would take my input, and I learned from him. We formed a great union; in fact, this approach to bringing work home and brainstorming together probably saved our relationship and gave him valuable insights into the business from a fresh female perspective. We had a stronger partnership and still we had "space." No one had a separate agenda.

I don't think your work should be this negative thing that you have to leave behind everyday. Even if you like your job, you don't have to shut off and turn on, then shut off again. You're not a light switch! Try bringing a little of your work home, talk about it, share it with your family *sometimes*. But for goodness' sake, don't dwell on it or vice versa. Let it go a little, too! I've integrated my kids into all aspects of my life, including my work. I recognize they have valuable advice to offer, just as Fred finally recognized what I had to offer. I just don't believe it's healthy to exempt people you love from vital parts of your life, and it's not healthy. Besides that, it's fun for us and makes great dinner table talk. One day the children will grow into adults, and these reflective times together will be valuable.

> *I don't think your work should be this negative thing that you have to leave behind everyday.*

MOMMY, CAN WE STILL
PAY THE MORTGAGE?

At the same time, there are healthy ways of inclusion. I'm not going to discuss rendering contracts with a seven-year old, for example. Just after Fred's death, when I was contemplating a more active role in the company, I discussed the potential change with my children. They gave me the thumbs up, not because they thought that's what I wanted, but because they truly felt that way. I encourage—respectfully encourage—free speech and thought in our home. That is important to note! But I noticed that my 10-year-old son, Freddie, was trying to be tough as the man of the house too fast when he tapped me on the shoulder one night and asked, "Mommy, can we still pay the mortgage?" After reassuring him that our days of living in Chevy vans were over, I realized that we have to let children be children. Involve them in our life but not our worries.

> Hypocrites make lousy parents. 'Do as I say, not as I do' just doesn't cut it.

Remember that children pick up so much from us, and they hear and see everything. As parents, we have the opportunity to make sure what they get are positive, empowering messages. But they may need our shoulder and hugs, encouragement, and explanations sometimes, too. Children are very bright and they do notice little things, like the tone of your voice and body language. Occasionally, a little acting and coaching may come in handy during a crunch. Always act from love for your babies; don't set out to deceive. Hypocrites make lousy parents. "Do as I say, not as I do" just doesn't cut it. Develop a keyword and send the kids off to school with it. Mine is "pride." We share a family slogan everyday. When I ask what does that mean, the kids answer,

"Take pride in everything you say and do today." "And what if you can't?" I ask. They answer in unison: "Then don't say or do it."

SING WITH ME, MOMMY

I don't believe in trying to "have it all," but I do believe it's possible to make a difference in the world by doing satisfying and fulfilling work while also being a good parent. For me, it's important to be accessible to my children. Thank goodness for cell phones! My kids can call me almost any time and I'll be at the other end of the phone to talk with them. I tell them I will check my messages after meetings or other times I have to shut down. I don't want to miss those precious moments when my children need me. Some of the cutest messages are interspersed between business jargon. It's nice. It can help them avert a crisis, or it can be about just giving them my attention when they need it. I don't freak out on them for not understanding how busy I am or guilt them about who puts the food on the table and a roof over your head baloney!

Like the time I was running for a plane recently and my phone rang. It was my baby girl. She had just learned to play "Hot Cross Buns" on her flute. "Sing with me, Mommy!" she urged. There I was, jogging through the airport, my cell phone cradled on one shoulder, pulling my carry-on, hair in a flurry, a briefcase on the other shoulder, singing "Hot Cross Buns": *One a-penny, two a-penny hot cross buns*—as my daughter played. I could care less about the funny looks I got! Psycho woman—let her through, I'm sure they thought.

> *I do believe it's possible to make a difference in the world by doing satisfying and fulfilling work while also being a good parent.*

More Tragedy and Triumph

The first year after Fred's untimely death was exhausting. I was on autopilot doing what needed to be done at work and at home, very robotic—trying to be perfect—everything to everybody. As a result, it seemed that everybody wanted a piece of me—my children, customers, suppliers, my executive team, and even the spirit world. My saving grace was my mother who selflessly cared for my children and provided me with so much support.

Then, six months after Fred's passing, I was hit with another cosmic two-by-four. I picked up the children from my mom's house at 4 P.M. one day. That evening, she suffered an aneurysm as a tornado ripped through town. Out of the blue, she died that night: another devastating loss for the children and me. She had helped me so much. Now I was barely treading water. I had to plan another funeral, balance my home with no babysitter, and my workload was huge. How could I go on, let alone be strong?

But I could finally see a light: Our dream was actually coming true. Our company was thriving. After we opened our expanded premises, productivity increased, we hired more people, and our customer base grew. The plan Fred and I developed together—grow aggressively to keep pace with our expanding customer base—was proving to be a winner. And as the world found out about the incredible Mitchell's story, a whole new chapter was unfolding in my fast-paced and totally crazy but blessed life. I caught my breath, spun around, and smiled for the cameras. The show must go on. Curtains, please. The next act was just beginning.

MY PLAN TO GET ME CLOSER TO MY DREAM:

Strengthen the company by expanding aggressively.

MY INSTINCTS:

Don't take the company public.

THE SEED FOR GOOD:

An outstanding strategic alliance with a major competitor gives Mitchell's the ability to expand.

Chapter Nine

LIFE LESSON:

Let Your Priorities Lead You

I make my way through the chaos of running a household and a business by identifying my priorities. I write down the things I simply must do that day, both business and personal. Try it—it's astonishing really to see how few things absolutely *must* get done on a certain day. Then I write down the other things I would like to do. But at the end of the day, I always take a minute to give myself credit for doing the "must" things and as many others as I achieve.

Why burden yourself with an endless to-do list that follows you from day to day—a constant source of guilt and irritation. Life isn't a contest to see how many tasks you can cross out on your to-do list. Don't get in the bad habit of beating yourself up. It is far more important to build yourself up.

*Mitchell succeeds
with the unexpected.*

— *Financial Post*, **2001**

As our business grew, so did my personal profile. For most of my adult life, I had been known as "Fred's wife." But after a couple of years at the helm of Mitchell's, balancing single parenting and a heavy workload, overseeing the strategic alliance with Schneiders, and launching our $44 million expansion, I became known as an entrepreneur in my own right.

A turning point was in September 2000 when I was named Canada's #1 Female Entrepreneur in a national competition. When that happened, I had a decision to make: Was I willing to go public with my story? This was an important decision because a high public profile can have a cost. I might have to worry about my family's privacy. I would have to re-live my past—both the triumphs and the tragedies. I had to figure out whether I would be able to pull seeds for good for the world out of it, or if it would just become another fiasco. I wondered about the children. As a mom, I could never do anything that may scar them for life. And to be true to myself and to Fred's memory, I would have to be completely honest and open. There are no skeletons in my closet—that's just not my style— even though the story does get a bit spooky at times.

I've never been one to let fear or threats stand in my way, and these considerations didn't deter me for long. I had a good talk with my best friend—me!—and I had a strong instinct that my story could help others. Once I started making honest and thought-provoking speeches to groups and doing media interviews, the response was overwhelming. People would come up to me after a speech and thank me for inspiring them to overcome a problem at work or home or even inside themselves—a struggle they faced or a push to pursue a dream. I got stacks of letters and e-mails from people across North America—then the world—telling me how my story had touched them. People would stop me at an airport, where at times I was on the cover of magazines on the stands, or a restaurant to say that I had helped them. I was immensely moved by their reaction. One woman mentioned that I looked better in person than on TV, but my jacket looked good on both spots! People are wonderful, aren't they? I was excited about the new door that was opening for me and the many beautiful people, places, and ideas I was exposed to as a result.

> *I was never one to let fear or threats stand in my way.*

LuAn Mitchell Named as One of the Leading Women Entrepreneurs of the World

Within a few months, I was named one of the 40 Leading Women Entrepreneurs of the World. What an experience to travel to Madrid, Spain and meet my fellow award winners. These successful women who are making a difference in the corporate world are a huge inspiration to me. I've become friends with some of these dynamic women—entrepreneurs like Margaret Jurca, an Australian real estate dynamo who has faced personal tragedy in her life. She was taken out of school at age 12. As a young woman, she was involved in a car accident that killed her only child and left Margaret badly injured. Then her husband left her. She recovered on all fronts and went on to start a real estate company whose sales today exceed one's wildest imaginations. When I see the diverse talents and tremendous energy at that international awards ceremony, I'm excited about the outstanding impact women are making in business all over the world.

As a very private and cautious person, one of the reasons I consent to being put in the public eye with award programs is to demonstrate to all aspiring entrepreneurs that we can make it. We must be there for each other, even against all odds, in the ever-so-scary eat 'em up and spit 'em out business world. I think when people read our stories and our triumphs and see women recognized as successful leaders consent to being put in the public eye with award programs, we demonstrate to all aspiring entrepreneurs that we can make it and become respected business professionals. Then more women see how they can also succeed, and they get the gentle push and encouragement to do it. We need to believe in each other and support and nurture each other every step along the way.

> *We must be there for each other, even against all odds, in the ever-so-scary, eat 'em up and spit 'em out business world.*

MITCHELL JOINS HARVARD BOARD

I'm living proof that a high school degree and a lot of hard work are enough to land you on a Board of one of the world's most prestigious universities. Although at university level I studied children's literature and psychology—even a bit of the arts, Fred's illness and my role as a caregiver prevented me from graduating. My business achievements caught the attention of Harvard University, and I was appointed to the Women's Leadership Board, a group that advises the John F. Kennedy School of Government about women's initiatives.

Again, this has been an opportunity to meet some fabulous, accomplished women—people like Anna Ouroumian. This young woman (she's not even 30!) has accomplished so much: first excelling academically at UCLA, then becoming a true leader in providing education opportunities to high potential, low opportunity youth. She turned around the non-profit Academy for Business Leadership in California, turning it into a powerful force for good by providing support for young people trying to stay in school. Anna's work is so similar to our efforts with the Fred Mitchell Memorial Scholarship Fund, and I am blessed to have the opportunity to meet inspiring people like her. My work with the Harvard board is like being surrounded by a tsunami and being pulled back into the most incredible high energy!

CANADA'S WOMAN ON TOP

As the headlines stacked up, so did the requests for speaking engagements. Meanwhile, I was still busy as Chair of Mitchell's Gourmet Foods. It was a busy time, but I was finally beginning to understand why I had undergone all these challenges—my teenage baby days, Fred's ill health, the family feud, putting my life on hold. All these allowed me to begin to design a world wherein I could exist to my full potential and highest good in as best as I could. They say our lives are God's gift to us; what we do with our lives is our gift back. I wanted to do justice to my gift. Although the corporate and personal difficulties were sometimes overwhelming, it was my calling to share my story with people, help them, and do good in the world. Yet another seed for good has been planted.

> *Our lives are God's gift to us; what we do with our lives is our gift back.*

Overcoming the Obstacles Women Face

Women have come a long way in the male-dominated business world. I recently read an article that claimed it's only a matter of time before women are running a substantial share of corporate America. What an exciting thought! In the meantime, we still face many obstacles in the business world. I've discovered a few strategies for succeeding in business as a woman.

The first thing is to do your homework. Know your stuff so people can't talk around or over you. It's important to be knowledgeable about your business, your competition, and industry trends. Read and surf the 'Net, looking for everything you can find that's relevant so you have the latest most updated knowledge. Stay abreast of the times; they can change rapidly. Get to know the financial side of business, and always be ethical. I was fortunate enough to have a business mentor who was all these things—my late husband Fred patiently taught me how to read a very complex production facility profit and loss statement, how to understand balance sheets, personal finances, follow trends, and much more. Don't let your lack of understanding of financial matters, or insecurities about learning, make you vulnerable to being ripped off. And don't let your lack of knowledge about your industry and its players put you in a position of weakness. A good and trustworthy accountant is invaluable, but you need to understand the details yourself or at the very least be available to discuss and formulate futures.

Second, don't make gender an issue. Don't get hung up on whether you are female or male because if you have something valuable to bring to the table, if you have the confidence required, you're capable and you've done your homework, it doesn't matter whether you're a man or a woman. Certainly, men and women can have very different styles. I notice how much men like joking and placing wagers. For instance, walking up to a bank of elevators with male colleagues, I wait for one of them to place a wager on which elevator is going to come first. It happens almost every time. Now I'm likely to jump in with a guess of my own. Why not join in the fun, maybe even win the little pot now and then, too. No harm done on small wagers like these.

Don't let your lack of understanding of financial matters, or insecurities about learning, make you vulnerable to being ripped off.

There have been lots of research about how the failure of women to engage in "guy talk" can prevent them from joining those informal networks that make it easier to advance in business. We need to get over the big divide between us. We should use our differences to strengthen each other. Harassment can go both ways—I have seen it, and I even worked once in a situation where a female co-worker thought she was in love with me and was relentless. As with most situations, I found that being upfront and blunt took care of the problem. It is a big world out there, so putting people in rigid categories is a big mistake.

It's also important to recognize that you will sometimes be

treated differently than a man would be in the same situation. After
the strategic alliance with Schneiders, part of our focus at Mitchell's
was to expand our customer base in
the food services industry. We believed
that one way to penetrate the big hotel
chains was to be accepted by some of
their jewel properties. In Western
Canada, a number of those jewel properties are located in Banff, Alberta. It
made good sense for Mitchell's to have

*It is a big world out there,
so putting people
in rigid categories
is a big mistake.*

a solid presence there. And what better way to show our commitment
to the food services industry than by having the company chair
based in Banff? In 1999, our family moved to Banff. The headline
in one newspaper reported it this way: "Mitchell uproots family, moves
to Banff." Can you imagine a male business leader getting the same
headline? No way! It would be reported as "New business comes to
Banff" or "Mitchell expands company operations." While I recognize
the occasional sexism in reporting, I just let it go. It's not a good use
of my energy to get irritated by this. *Worry about what you can control,*
I tell myself.

Don't Blend in with the Crowd

My third strategy for women to succeed in the business world
is to remain true to yourself no matter what. When women were
making inroads in the business world in the 1980s, you could decipher their strategy just by looking at them. Remember the dress
for success "business suit"? We even wore little silk ties—the
Victor Victoria look! And remember the big hair, Farrah Fawcett beau-
ties? Bring on the spray! Women were trying to look like stiff female
versions of men. What are you really contributing if you aren't being
yourself developing your own individual style but instead mimicking

someone else? I like to think that today, women are more comfortable being themselves in the business world. I have no problem wearing a bright red, pink, or even orange jacket or sweater. I don't own a boxy male cut, pinstripe, starched navy suit—it's just not me.

The important thing is to wear clothing that makes you feel good, is your style, and helps you do your job comfortably. Be professional, but be yourself.

My third strategy for women to succeed in the business world is to remain true to yourself no matter what.

Another important place to "keep it professional" yet smart business is on your business card. One of our wedding gifts was extraordinary and came with a business card. The gift was his and hers handmade jewelry items. The business card included stated "the women who wear and treasure these from generation to generation." Well, that was okay for my piece of jewelry, but the jewelry for my husband was gorgeous and forgotten in the message on the card. Be careful.

I feel strongly that women should be unafraid to demonstrate their natural nurturing instincts and creative genius as leaders. These are common characteristics that most women execute well and very few men have or execute at all. We have the ability to create a more supportive and family-oriented work environment. But we sometimes still have to draw the line between our business and personal lives. As a former single woman in the business world, I've had a few romantic overtures from business associates and acquaintances. My approach was to be absolutely clear that this business relationship was not

Don't be afraid to be up front: Respect yourself and people will respect you for it.

going to become a personal relationship. Don't be afraid to be up front: Respect yourself and people will respect you for it. You can be frank in a professional way so that no one takes offense.

How Do You Do It?

I can't tell you how many times people have come up to me after a presentation and asked, "How do you do it? How do you do your work, raise your children, and stay sane?" "Easy," I answer, "I'm not sane—I'm really nuts!" Just joking actually. Keeping your sense of humor is critical! My answer is that generally, it's a constant balancing act—it's tough, no lie. Sometimes, there aren't enough hours in the day. I try to remain flexible; things will undoubtedly always come up. If you have to shift a few things, let it go. It can really take the wind out of your sail if you don't accomplish too many unnecessary things on an overloaded list, and that's just dumb. It's much more rewarding and effective to focus on your priorities than to carry forward an enormous, unrealistic "to do" list everyday that serves to drain your energy and bring you down.

If you've ever had a demanding job, you know how easy it is to devote virtually all your time and energy to work. Lots of people do it—this or that form of an "aholic" behavior. And we've all seen the results—their health, personal relationships, and happiness often suffer. There aren't enough 12-step programs out there for them all. We've all been in attendance at an organ recital. Oh, my aching this, my aching that. He's my pain in the !?!!? You know what I mean!

I've never been one to continuously work 70-hour weeks because I started having children at a fairly young age. But when I used to stress, I stressed hard! I took it very seriously. I took everything very seriously. As a matter of fact, I took everything very seriously to my detriment until I learned better. Late hours and sleepless nights used to come easy for me. It seems I've always had my kids to keep me balanced or keep me awake to remind me of the importance of my personal life and my responsibility to them as well.

Work is important, but it is not everything. Remember that some things have to give or you risk some very precious commodities; you can't turn the clock back! One day when I was on my first month of very little sleep, my little girl asked me: "What are those lines between your nose and mouth?"

"Oh those are laugh lines, honey," I answered.

She looked at me puzzled and said, "But Mommy, you're not laughing, and they're still there."

They say we have the face God gave us until 25, then after that we have the face we gave ourselves! Be careful—looking hard may work if you're Clint Eastwood, but this is the real world and not Hollywood.

Defining Balance for Yourself

A balanced lifestyle means different things for different people. You need to devise for yourself a definition of balance—that point where you're comfortable, productive, and stabilized. The important thing is to recognize that we all have several important areas in our life. In addition to work, there are our family and friends, exercise, personal growth and learning, meal preparation, downtime, and the spiritual side of our lives—to name a few. You should try to devote some time every week to each part of your life. Plan it just as you would a business meeting.

I schedule in a workout several times a week because it's just as important to me as a major customer meeting or a board meeting. But that meant a little space set aside in my home, some light weights, and a mat so I can get up extra early, put time in, shower, get the kids off to school then start the rest of my work day. It took some serious planning. I often go to bed shortly after I put the kids down, earlier than I'd like, but I feel healthier. And during my morning workout, I use the time to listen to motivational tapes or catch up on the news—local or CNN—that I missed the night before. When I finish my workout, I feel energetic, empowered, and ready to meet any challenge the day has for me. A fresh air power walk is invigorating also.

Figure out what some of your personal priorities or just plain old wish list items are, and add them to your schedule. Juggle around a few things if you must. Ten years from now, you'll remember your child's school play and smile with pride, or a family hike that gave you that little scar on your "leg of stories" more than those extra hours you spent straining away at your desk or rolling around on those sleepless worry nights. What are you really achieving if you are plagued with guilt internally because you are missing an important time in one of your children's lives, or you haven't done any meaningful physical activity for weeks?

> *You need to devise for yourself a definition of balance—that point where you're comfortable, productive, and stabilized.*

WHAT'S YOUR PASSION?

How do you function when you are inspired? I think we all embrace life more fully and use our talents more effectively when we are stirred by something. I have many passions—dogs (I have a handful of them), reading (I'm passionate about learning and always have a couple of books on the go), and art. I am fortunate to have the means to indulge my love of art and fill my house with awe-inspiring pieces.

I am inspired by artists like Norval Morrisseau (sometimes called the Canadian Picasso)—not just for his fantastic art, but also the story of this artist who battled addiction and went from skid row to huge critical acclaim. I own several of Morrisseau's paintings, and they fill my house with a wonderful energy. My taste runs from huge jade carvings from Native artists to Dresden china from dynasty eras. I have a magnificent bronze statue in my living room, Hiawatha of Iroquois. I think of this legendary chief and leader as a mentor. With his Iroquois haircut, chain dangling down his forehead, and pierced ears, he is very "now" and would be right at home in any current music video!

As our journey progresses, there are always new discoveries—and some of the most interesting are discoveries about ourselves. For instance, have you ever Googled your own name? When my maiden name is typed into the computer, it leads to the myth of Gingara—a totally new discovery for me and mentoring from a different angle. The myth of Gingara comes from Buddhism in the Himalayas. There's real pride in family name here. The myth holds that the Gingara—a creature half woman and half bird—descends a ladder made of jewels to bring good fortune to all living creatures on planet Earth. The mythical creature is a representation of positive thoughts during an annual three month retreat important to the Buddhist religion—and is depicted by a peacock in the celebrations.

I share my love of art with two interesting men—Fred Mendel, who founded a major art gallery in Western Canada and my husband Reese's father, Aubrey Halter. As destiny would have it, those two men were once in negotiations over a Modigliani painting Aubrey owned. After seeing it featured in *Architectural Digest* (those headlines again!), Fred Mendel discussed acquiring the painting, though he ultimately did not purchase it.

THE TUNNEL OF LOVE

Another form of art in my home is what I refer to as my "Tunnel of Love." In our basement, there is a long hallway that is absolutely covered in family photos going years back. These photos are more precious to me than any expensive piece of art. If a fire broke out in my home, those photos would be the first possession I would try to save. The important thing is to know what inspires you. Whether it's art, poetry, fresh flowers, family photos, music, special books, or a collection of figurines, we always need to surround ourselves with things and people we admire and that bring us joy and have meaning. We all know of things and people that speak to our soul. Make them part of your life and soak up their marvelous energy.

> *We all know of things and people that speak to our soul. Make them part of your life and soak up their marvelous energy.*

Don't Try to Do It All Alone

Always remember that you have options to help you cope with all of life's obligations. Consider hiring someone to do your books if you are on overload, clear up the administrative backlog, or even just wash your windows. Mary Kay Ash used to tell her sales force that they shouldn't spend their time scrubbing their floors when they could be out selling: "You're spending one-dollar time on a one-cent chore." I couldn't get along without the people who help me with jobs like cleaning. I have brought to life two of my childhood comic friends, Betty and Veronica, who now help me with my house and children. (Those are their real names—honest!) I don't know what I would do without them; they are great at their jobs and a huge asset to this world! Honor those people, pay them fairly, and treat them respectfully. If you're one of them, do the best job you can do. You are valuable and probably not thanked enough.

Life Will Get Out of Balance Sometimes. Get Over It.

It's also important to remember that the scales will change. If there's a week where my children are dancing in a show, performing in a school play, competing at a golf tournament, or skiing down a mountain, I'll dedicate more time to them and spend less time writing, reading reports, or staying late at the office. Sometimes, my speaking engagements, board meetings, work or seminars will require me to be away from home for several days at a time. I've learned that sometimes life is just going to be out of whack. I accept this as normal and natural but not the way it's going to be locked in forever. Nothing is written in stone. We all get busy; we all experience stormy seas. And that's fine, as long as we know and remember to apply strategies to get back to reality and back on course. Don't be afraid to speak honestly and openly with the ones you love when things get out of sync. You can say with sincerity: "I'm sorry." You're going to miss the mark once or twice on both sides of your balancing act; perfection is not the goal, balance is.

> *Perfection is not the goal, balance is.*

DO YOU HAVE WHAT IT TAKES TO SURVIVE?

Taking risks can be a great character-building exercise. I discovered this again in the spring of 2000 when I took part in a four-day survival trek through the Utah desert. The opportunity arose after I appeared on *The Hour of Power* with my dear friend and mentor Dr. Robert Schuller in California. As I was leaving Orange County, my cell phone rang. It was the editor of *Self* magazine. A colleague of hers had just heard me speak, she told me. She was looking for women who "swim with the sharks," so to speak—women who would take part in a grueling survival trek. She thought I'd be perfect. As she explained the experience—four

> *Taking risks can be a great character-building exercise.*

days hiking through the desert, no food, no water, time solo, severe conditions—my excitement grew. By the end of that first phone call, I had agreed to do it. How weird is that? Believe me, there was no million dollars in it either!

It just felt right but first I had to get the okay from my most trusted advisors—my children. I explained that this trek would be challenging but that mommy felt something wonderful calling her to do it. Their response was, "Go for it, Mom." Next I met with my lawyer. When he read the liability waiver *Self* magazine sent, he looked at me in astonishment. "Why do you want to do this? We are not just your lawyers, LuAn, we are also your friends. Is everything okay?" he asked. The waiver outlined in great detail all the dangers that could imperil me—from falling off a cliff to being bitten by a scorpion—and made it clear I was liable for anything that happened to me. I also needed to make it clear in writing that my estate could not sue. I explained that this was something I really wanted to do and that I intended to do it. "Fine," my lawyer said. Then he found the silver lining in the cloud: "At least it's a well-written waiver!"

Certainly, I felt some doubts deep down. I thought, *Is this what a widow with three young children should be doing?* But I felt a tremendous sense of excitement about the experience. It just kept bubbling up inside! When I really listened to myself, I heard that this could be a once-in-a-lifetime experience. And that's pretty irresistible to a girl like me.

Our adventure began when we met in Salt Lake City. As I was going through United States Customs, I was questioned about the purpose of my trip. When I explained, the customs officer got worried, "Are you sure you know these people?" This is how people get abducted, not to mention the fact that I had a big knife in my suitcase. I would be up the creek now trying that stunt! My resolve was really being tested. I was nervous, and I'm sure it showed. My fellow survivors were Liz, a black belt karate expert who has trained NYPD officers; Dyan, a corporate lawyer; and Maria, a tough reporter for the *New York Post*. (I was billed as "slaughterhouse owner" in her subsequent magazine article!)

Alone and Unequipped in the Desert

The organizers searched us when we finally drove out to our remote destination and confiscated our usual survival gear—watches, wallets, cell phones, beepers, jewelry, and Maria's cigarettes. I had searched out and subsequently stashed all kinds of wonderful high tech wilderness equipment—biodegradable toilet paper, a cardboard port-a-potty, and snake venom sucker. But the organizers found my contraband and took it as well—cést la vie.

In return, we were allowed an enamel cup, our big knife, and a compass. Then we were set loose in the dark and creepy Utah desert in the middle of the night. The coyotes were howling, and we were finding our way over the rough terrain by the light of the full moon. I was scared of the scorpions, snakes, and other creatures that lurked out there—nocturnal buddies I would just as soon never know! But I was probably more scared of a close encounter of another kind. The locals told us the area was known as a UFO landing strip, so I was constantly watching the sky for strange lights. And it didn't help when one of the tough women pointed out that escaped convicts would consider this the perfect place to hide out—nice thought!

We spent the next four days hiking up mountains, through rivers, over cliffs, and through canyons as well as forests of dried out bristle. We endured excruciating heat during the day—the month was June—and bone-chilling cold sleeping on rocks at night. Whenever we hit a river, we'd drink as much as we could. We had no time to boil it for purification. If we'd be walking for a while with no water and we'd find an old rain puddle, we'd dip our cup in the murky sludge and just drink it. It tasted vile but it helped us avoid dehydration, which could have been deadly, and rainwater, even if shared with a lizard, is a lot better than the other stuff. For a moment, I just couldn't believe that I ever sent back a drink in a restaurant because there was a speck of something or other in it, or the glass was dirty— God forbid!

One of the first lessons I learned was about the importance of doing your homework before a trip like this: Don't just take the clerk's advice. I didn't research what kind of hiking boots to wear. I just assumed a pair of good, strong Canadian leather hiking boots like the ones we wear in Banff would be best. Boy, did I pay for that assumption. Once my practical and healthy boots got wet, they became heavy bogging me down and took forever to dry. For most of the trek, I felt like I was hiking with cement blocks on my swollen and aching feet. I even had to sleep in these heavy, wet gross boots one night. If I took them off, I'd never get my tender, swollen, and blistering feet back into them. Talk about feeling like Cinderella's ugly stepsister. I knew why *Charlie's Angels* wear heels everywhere. This was no Hollywood scene from a movie: This was the outback at its finest.

Ant Larvae—Yum!

After two days with no food, we were starting to see black spots flash before our eyes, a sign that our bodies desperately needed protein. We tried to catch fast-moving fish in the rivers with our bare hands like bears but didn't even come close to succeeding. We had been instructed how to catch a scorpion, remove the stinger, and eat it raw, but we weren't that desperate yet! We started digging for big, juicy ant larvae. It's pretty simple: You just find an anthill and dig and burrow until you find the larvae. Popping them in the hatch and eating them was the tough part. I just squeezed my eyes shut and gulped them down, swallowing hard with my dry throat, feeling the lump as it slid its way down. There was no chaser to wash it down, and no wormy tequila to lighten the mood. They actually tasted a bit like Rice Krispies—or maybe I was just hallucinating! I will never know, as there will be no revisiting the moment soon!

> *It's really not that difficult to find something to complain about no matter what situation you are in if that is your mindset. But it's never worth it.*

We're Our Own Worst Enemies

But our biggest challenge wasn't the forbidding terrain, the mind-numbing hunger, or the dangers that lurked in the desert. It appeared to be the group dynamics. Things came to a head on or around the second day. We started to argue about whether we should continue up a steep mountain or stop for the night. We were brand new at this, exhausted, hungry, and sore. Tempers flared. Although we had only known each other for a short time, the comments got personal. We were at each other's throats for about two hours, wasting a lot of precious energy and time. But we eventually figured it out. We had to; we needed each other too much. It's strange to think that we posed more of a challenge to each other than the desert did—at that moment in time, at least.

This powerful experience was another lesson for me: When people you're working with get personal and nasty, stay away from getting sucked in. By falling victim, you start devoting your energy and precious time to something negative rather than constantly moving toward your goal. It's easy to criticize, gossip, and snipe at people—there will be plenty of opportunities. Trust me. It's really not that difficult to find something to complain about no matter what situation you are in if that is your mindset. But it's never worth it. Stand apart from the water cooler chitchat. Those won't be the long-lasting relationships in your life. Yes, some people look better going than coming, but there is no need to make a big production about it! Keep some class. Keep your head down and stay focused on your own priorities. It's all right to realize that some people are able to hit where it hurts—but be bigger than that.

> Stand apart from the water cooler chitchat. Those won't be the long-lasting relationships in your life.

If we didn't have that mid-mountain argument, we would probably have had enough energy to get to the top of any mountain we needed to cross, but there was no need to go to the limit. It turned out to be a big misunderstanding about whether there was food at the top: There was none! Then we tried to get some sleep for a fresh start in the morning. As it was, we had to calm down and rebuild energy.

Overcoming Fear

The scariest part of the trek was probably the solo—a day and a night completely on my own. Alone and lost, I felt emotional and jittery as the sun set. I sat quietly on the edge of a cliff listening to the music of the desert, absolutely enraptured. I'd see the outline of small nocturnal furry rat-like creatures scurry past me, and my imagination was running wild. But after a while, the fear subsided and a feeling of peace took over. Your body simply can't keep the adrenaline going for that long.

When I decided to tune back in to the wonder of nature, I stopped being a scared and edgy woman, and I started to fall in love with the wonder of the desert. I began to realize that when we're forced to, we can survive things we didn't think we could. When you really have to dig deep down, you find reserves of strength and dignity you never knew you had. It's like finding a drawer of treasures that you've never opened. When you pull the handle, you discover it is full of precious things you never knew you had. What an exhilarating discovery. The lovely radio of the desert was my lullaby that night, and the little purring and buzzing creatures my friends. I surrendered my heart and mind and became eternally thankful for our time together: I decided I would not give in to fear and its captors and be robbed of this experience!

You don't need to go to the Utah desert to discover your inner strength. The most important thing is to get out of your self-imposed comfort zone every once in a while. Challenge yourself. Go somewhere totally different. Learn something new. Above all, take risks, and don't gripe. When the stakes are high and you face the possibility of real danger, your senses are heightened and you truly feel alive. In stories about the desert trek, *Self* magazine and the *New York Post* paid me a wonderful

> I began to realize that when we're forced to, we can survive things we didn't think we could.

> The most important thing is to get out of your self-imposed comfort zone every once in a while.

compliment saying, "LuAn Mitchell is that almost-unheard of thing: a woman boss in the macho world of meat processing. She's developed eyes in the back of her head to keep her company from being hijacked by a corporate raider, and she has the cast-iron stomach needed to ride herd over her company's kill and cut floor." Hey, now, that's what its all about: Never judge by appearances. Go get 'em, Tiger!

Not All Risks Are Created Equal

There are certain risks not worth taking. The one thing I wouldn't risk is family unity. I've seen and been a part of a family torn apart, and I won't let that happen to anyone else if I can help it. Otherwise, I'm just as willing to take risks today as I was when we were fighting to save our corporate family. It wouldn't be my first choice to live in an old broken down van again. But if I was fighting for something I believed in, you'd better believe I'd do it—and more.

> Don't let age be your cage.

And my children are no different. When I talk to them about potential projects, they often say, "Go for it, Mom! You can do it!" Don't let age be your cage. I want to be a good example to them, not a stick-in-the-mud-mom.

That kind of encouragement and support is essential for risk-takers. There are stories of entrepreneurs whose appetite for risk far exceeded their spouse's comfort level. Ray Kroc of McDonald's fame went through a divorce shortly after quitting his job to devote himself to his new fast-food business. His wife thought a man approaching 60 years of age should be planning for retirement, not taking a flyer on an unproven business.

On the other hand, there are people like Rosalie Sharp. When her husband, fledgling hotelier Issy Sharp took Rosalie to the proposed location for the second Four Seasons Hotel in the early 1960s, Rosalie took one look at the barren location on the outskirts of Toronto and resigned herself to losing everything they owned and having to go back to work. But she didn't say anything. Pregnant with her fourth child, she was willing to share this risk with her husband. Fortunately, she didn't stop Issy from following his impassioned blueprint and eventually becoming one of the world's leading luxury hoteliers.

You have to realize that risk is a funny thing. When Fred was trying to arrange his heart/double lung transplant, several very reputable and well-meaning doctors told him not to do it because he was so sick they thought he'd never make it. They said he would be wise to just be content with what time he had left. But what did they know (even if they meant well)? That risk paid off—he had eight more glorious years of wonderful life and two more miraculous children.

How do you know if you should take a particular risk? Whose advice is the right advice? Sometimes, people ask me whether they should take a chance with a certain kind of business. My response is that if they felt a mission, if they felt passionate about it, they'd probably be out there doing it, not talking about it. It's like the story of the hound dog on the porch that lay there howling all day and all night. Someone asked his owner what was wrong. "He's lying on a rusty nail," the owner explained. "Why doesn't he get up?" the visitor asked. The owner replied, "Oh, he will when it hurts enough."

Start making some changes; don't spend all your time and energy second-guessing yourself.

If you're lying on a rusty nail, get up for goodness' sake! Start making some changes; don't spend all your time and energy second-guessing yourself. If you have to stop and ask too many people questions, you should take that as a sign that you might be in the wrong place or going in the opposite direction, perhaps a little off course even.

Another risk I'm increasingly wary of is getting caught up in the spirit of a deal. There's a tendency to want a deal or goal so badly that you'll do anything to get it, rush in, or do what I like to call a "knee-jerk reaction." If you want something at any price, someone, somewhere will recognize this desire and could take advantage of you. You'll get ripped off if they do. I try to stay detached, take an aerial view of the deal-making, and be ready to walk away from a deal if someone is negotiating in bad faith.

I was recently looking at purchasing a property I loved. In my research, I saw that the place had been taken off the market and then put back on a year later. It was purchased for a lot less and then jacked up to ridiculous proportions. I put in what I thought was a reasonable offer for the track record. The seller's rude response was to ****** off. The karma was all wrong, and I walked. Nothing is worth that!

From Tragedy to Top of the World

While I talk about taking risks, I have to admit that I wasn't ready to risk dating for a long time after Fred's death. With a huge company to run, three young children to raise (not to mention five dogs, an iguana, a turtle, and fish), and a busy household to maintain, the last thing I had time for was dating. I told myself someone who demands my time, butts into my family ways, and gets hurt feelings— "not going to happen." I was pretty surprised when I got whacked by another cosmic two-by-four.

Our family was on holiday in beautiful Hawaii, attending the Maui Writers' Conference in tropical Maui. I always appreciated the opportunity to learn from publishers and authors at these events and mingle. On the last day of our holiday, I was eating breakfast with my daughter Jinji. "There's a nice looking guy over there," said Jinji. Thinking she spied some fourth grader, I paid little attention and remained totally absorbed in my coffee and newspaper. Then she put a plumeria flower behind her ear and walked past her cutie to get some juice.

Next thing I knew, I looked around to see Jinji and this handsome young man chatting. When I looked at him, I saw a bright beautiful light around him. It shone like the sun, and I was taken aback. That had only happened once before in my life—when Fred Mitchell came back to life after his transplant. The first time he opened up his eyes, the light was amazing. That morning in Hawaii, I quickly discounted it as too much sun and went back to my coffee. Then when my daughter didn't return, I walked over to his table.

"Oh, hi," he said in a great strong voice, "are you her mom?"

"Yes, I am" I answered, taking Jinji by her hand.

"I'm a children's book author, and I wanted to send her a book," he explained.

I gave him my business card. "Send it here then, thanks," I responded, having just met so many wonderful authors. Then the children and I headed to the beach.

Getting ready to go to the beach that day was another of life's learning moments. I was fussing over whether to wear my cover-up over my bathing suit. I still had scars on my leg from a fall during my Utah desert trek and thought I should cover them up. "Don't do that," said my son Ryan. "That's your leg of stories! Everybody should have one." I realized he was right and I ditched the cover-up, proudly displaying my leg of stories.

A few weeks later, my assistant said this guy, a tree biologist and scientist, was calling, asking if Jinji got his book. It turns out it was a delightful story about Bruni the Bear that taught children about tree ecology. This guy, Reese, was asking me out to dinner, Judy added. I accepted, and pretty soon we were dating.

When I got to know Dr. Reese, I couldn't believe this kind, smart, generous man was on earth. It took me a while but then I knew why I saw the beautiful light around him. I couldn't believe that I had fallen in love again. In this world of Internet dating and agencies, I just needed my little girl to discover the most wonderful man for me. And Reese's dad, Aubrey, was on the job, too. A distinguished and thoughtful man in his mid-80s, he had faxed his son a newspaper ad that promoted one of my speaking engagements. "Perhaps you should ask her out," Aubrey suggested. Reese received the fax the day he arrived home from Maui. He studied the photo in the ad and then called his dad in New York. "I just met her in Maui," Reese told him. Just like the newspaper photo that caught Fred Mitchell's eye so many years before, living my life in the headlines was working to my advantage again. Coincidences like this only serve to strengthen my belief in God!

In addition to being a bestselling children's author, Reese is a respected scientist and lover of the earth. Our relationship, like most, hit some bumps in the early days. Reese was a 37-year-old bachelor—just as Fred was when we met, oddly enough. I give Reese lots of credit for working hard to figure out my feisty, outspoken children; and cautious, distant me. We certainly gave him a rough ride at times. One time, his staff placed some of my past headlines across their boss's desk to freak him out. But he hung in there and became part of our family. The day he proposed to me was one of the happiest days of my life. I was ready for the fairy tale wedding and the happily-ever-after ending. I should have known it wouldn't be that simple.

MY PLAN TO GET ME CLOSER TO MY DREAM:

Use my experience to help others.

MY INSTINCTS:

It's worth taking the risk of being in the spotlight.

THE SEED FOR GOOD:

The reaction of people who are inspired by my story.

Chapter Ten

LIFE LESSON:

Protect Your Power

Since our wedding, several people have asked why I didn't stand up and refute the points made in the newspaper ad that ran on my wedding day. The ad was quoted in newspaper stories across the country—reporters were only too happy to serve up the salacious details of the Mitchell family feud again. This has happened to me many times before. After giving interviews to reporters and authors, I am sometimes shocked at the errors, mistakes, and distortions that are published.

It's so tempting to fight back, but it's not a good use of my time and energy. I couldn't control what was said, but I could choose how to respond. If I got into a fight about this, I would be giving away my power. By taking the high road and maintaining my focus on what's important to me—my new husband, my family, advancing good in the world any way I can, and my important work—I could continue to enjoy a reality of love, happiness, and gratitude.

Wedding goes on despite family feud.

— *National Post*, December 4, 2002

My wedding to Reese was planned for November 2002. We would get married at the historic and beautiful Fairmont Banff Springs Hotel, a real castle in our hometown of Banff. Reese and I had so much fun planning our big day. Jinji wanted to sing, my bridesmaids would wear fabulous red dresses with white silk shawls, and all our family and friends would be there. It was going to be perfect.

The afternoon before the wedding, as our guests started arriving in Banff, my executive assistant and beautiful sister Judy received a phone call from a reporter with one of Canada's national newspapers. The reporter told her that Fred's sister had taken out a large (and very costly) ad in tomorrow's newspaper, apparently implying that I had distorted the truth about what happened in Fred's family feud six years earlier. Would I like to respond? Sure enough, the ad was in the newspaper on our wedding day. I didn't respond then, and I haven't responded since. The reason is simple: I refuse to take the bait. I won't waste precious time speculating on why someone would choose to place such an ad at all, let alone on that particular day—my wedding day. I won't be drawn into a negative debate over past events and rehashing the sacred memories of dead people.

> *I won't be drawn into a negative debate over past events.*

At our wedding, reporters asked me again to respond to the large ad, now out in all its glory in the paper. "People have certain realities, and they are entitled to them," I told the reporters. "Today our reality is love and forgiveness, and I wish that for everybody. I hope our happiness is infectious." Then the bridal party entered the reception, and we went on to have the most fabulous fairy tale wedding I could have ever imagined. Reese was particularly sensitive to my pain and squeezed my hand. His family was kind and good to the children and me. His brother shared a tear-jerking talk with the group, and his sister, who is an accomplished musician, took our son Fred for a walk. They talked about the power of music to heal. All three children performed at the ceremony—it was truly special on a higher level.

> *People have certain realities, and they are entitled to them.*

And as always, I found a seed for good in this event. When the ad ran on our wedding day, I got so many beautiful expressions of support. For example, the head of our union at Mitchell's followed up by praising me in a newspaper article. Reese's family was sensitive, kind, and welcoming. And my true friends gathered around, determined that my wedding day would be a happy event—which it was.

The Zen Monks

Two Zen monks resting beside a river saw a beautiful woman on the other side of the river. She asked them to help her cross the river. This was a problem because they were not allowed to touch women. The monks thought of how they could help her cross the river without touching her. They couldn't carry her or cross their hands to form a seat—that would be touching her. They thought for a long time and couldn't come up with a solution. Finally, one monk just waded across the river, picked up the woman and carried her across. Then the two monks continued on their walk. For the next hour, the one monk berated the other.

"You've just broken every taboo to help that woman! We've worked so hard to reach this point of ascension and you've ruined it. How could you do it?" On and on he ranted. Finally, the first monk said, "I put that woman down an hour ago. Why are you still carrying her?"

Are you still carrying some negative baggage? In my van days, my bags (luggage) were garbage bags. Today, I like Louis Vuitton. But hey, it's all about the load inside! We will all be the victims of unpleasant events. We can't control many of those events. But we can control how and what we react to and then pack into our bags, garbage, or otherwise. Allow yourself to forgive others and yourself, and enjoy the liberating feeling of letting go of negative energy.

> *Allow yourself to forgive others and yourself, and enjoy the liberating feeling of letting go of negative energy.*

I HAVE ANOTHER MOM

I have been working hard on forgiveness ever since my teenage pregnancy. I was lucky enough to meet my daughter Jaki in the most unexpected way. After Fred's transplant, I was worn out and run down from the stress and demands of nursing a very ill man. At one point, Fred's doctor suggested that I take a break—it would do me good, and it would lessen Fred's dependence on me. I decided to go back to Saskatchewan and asked the tourist board for some suggestions for a quiet, pretty place. They suggested Radville, a small town in southern Saskatchewan, and I thought, "Why not?"

It was just a short trip, but I contacted the local school and offered to come read some children's fiction I had written. After the reading, I had a chance to chat with some of the children. One pretty little girl sidled up to me and whispered, "I have a secret."

"Oh, what's that?" I asked, as I could see she wanted me to.

"I have another mom," the little angel confessed. Well, one thing led to another and pretty soon she was sharing her birth date with me. I almost fell over when I realized this was my little "Jacqueline." This was no coincidence; this was God allowing me to set things right. I was thrilled to see that she was thriving and living happily with the family who had adopted her. We corresponded once I got back to California, and she even lived with Fred, the children, and me for a time. Although Jaki went through some tough times as a sometimes-rebellious teenager (just like her birth mom), she is now a lovely young woman. And I feel at peace with my difficult decision all those years ago.

Whether it's about forgiving yourself or forgiving others, sometimes

> Sometimes the best action is to put down your sword and quit the fight.

the best action is to put down your sword and quit participating in the fight. If it's a choice between surrounding myself with positive energy or negative energy, I know which way I'll turn every time. I'm proud of where I've been and what I've done. Life is definitely stranger than fiction sometimes. I'm very comfortable and happy in my own skin and believe that is why I can enjoy the many gifts in my life.

Wicked Queen Anger Management

I have a favorite T-shirt that I often wear at speaking engagements. It shows the nasty queen from Snow White and has the caption: "Wicked Queen Anger Management. Don't like what you see in the mirror? Call us!" I think this carries a powerful message in a humorous way. If you don't like what you see when you look in the mirror, don't go around giving people poisoned apples. Change and adapt yourself until you like what you see. Let other people off the hook.

> *We all need to recognize that we're not going to get along with every person we meet.*

I have no enemies; I refuse to get sucked into that duality. In fact, I pray for many people, including *those whom I feel have wronged me*. I choose to see *them* as creative people with many gifts, *and* I want *them to be happy*. I have seen miracles—I believe *everyone* is entitled to one, too!

We all need to recognize that we're not going to get along with every person we meet. But that doesn't mean these people have to be enemies. To give in to that kind of thinking is to give up my power. I need my power to remain peaceful, nurture my family, and do whatever good I can in this world at every turn.

Our Family's Secret Weapon

Raising a family is a challenge at the best of times, but Fred and I emphasized being open and honest with our children from when they were babies. He believed that lack of communication in his family set the stage for their tragic falling out. When the children were young, we began holding family meetings. These happen most Sunday evenings. The rules are simple: You can speak for seven minutes (we have a designated timekeeper), you can use whatever emotional language you want, and there are no taboos. It is a safe zone. We do not judge each other during this time together. This is how we keep the lines of communication open. Sometimes, the meetings are short and simple; sometimes, they are fiery and emotional. But we are always completely frank, and we always wind up with hugs, realizing it is the situations and not the people we are upset with. We are happy to explore each other.

These meetings have been my family's salvation. Whether it's a crisis or a cause for celebration, we all know when it's time for a family gathering. My new husband was bombarded when he met my family, but his willingness to embrace our family meetings was one way he passed the test with both my kids and me.

My turbulent, but absolutely fabulous, Banff wedding signaled the beginning of yet another new chapter in my life. I could sense that as one dream began—my marriage to Reese—another dream was reaching fruition. My mission with Mitchell's was now complete. It was time to move on. Time to pack my bags and hit the road: A new journey had begun.

MY PLAN TO GET ME CLOSER TO MY DREAM:

Live in my own reality.

MY INSTINCTS:

Don't get sucked into other people's negativity.

THE SEED FOR GOOD:

Renewed support from family and friends.

Chapter Eleven

LIFE LESSON:

Giving Back Offers Tremendous Rewards

I strongly believe that if we can give back to our community, we should. And it's not just about big donations. When I was in my early 20s, I coached an inner city baseball team. I saw these girls who wanted to play, who needed to stay out of trouble, but didn't have a coach. Volunteering to be their coach was a fantastic experience.

Since then, I have volunteered for dozens of business and community groups. Now I'm in a position where I can also offer money to worthy causes. And I do. But giving back isn't always about money—it's mostly about giving of *yourself*. And I've always found that you get back tenfold what you give. It can really be very simple to plant a seed for good.

Stepping into
a new spotlight.

— Profit magazine, October 2001

When I look back on my life, I realize I've come yearning to have my voice heard. When I made my ill-fated women's lib speech at the Miss Canada pageant, I was just trying to be heard. But I didn't have a story to tell yet. Maybe that's why I had to endure so many challenges—nursing a chronically ill husband, enduring an acrimonious family feud, nursing a sick company back to health, and watching as my husband took his last breath. Now that's a story to tell! My new career, as a platform speaker, is tremendously satisfying. And I finally have the opportunity to give back to the causes that are important to me. From that first speech at the pageant, I've come full circle. Now people listen to my speeches!

> I was just trying
> to be heard.
> But I didn't have
> a story to tell yet.

LuAn Mitchell Sells Her Stake in Mitchell's

Once Mitchell's was humming along and steadily building its customer base, I realized that our dream had come true. Fred and I planned so long for this moment—when our company would be so vibrant that no one would think of trying to shut it down. I had made a promise to Fred. When he died and I kissed his swollen, medicated cheek, I had my butterfly vision and made the ultimate deal. For as we think so shall it be done, I decided I had to see our dream through. And I had.

"What was I thinking?" I raked my brain for a recall of my thoughts. There were so many changes and innovations that I was proud of. Our wonderful Peer Support program. Our fantastic robot, Jack the Ribber. A growing customer base. Progressive employment programs. Sure we still had challenges, but the time of crises had passed.

Then I remembered what I was thinking! It was Helen Reddy. The melody flooded my senses. I rooted through my old audiotapes. There she was. I popped it on my stereo, my cassette played, I cranked it loud—I danced like never before! *I am woman hear me roar in {voices} too big to ignore!* Yes, that was it: Our people were secure, our company was intact—bigger and better then it ever was. We had completed the largest expansion in our history. All the right pegs were in all the right peg holes, and I was starting a new life with a man I love. My kids were healthy and happy in our new home in our new town. It was time to breathe life into the next phase of the dream.

I put my right arm in the air, clenched my fist, and pulled it down proudly exclaiming our triumph! While Helen belted it out— *I'm still an embryo with a long, long way to go!*—a perfect birth had prevailed! The memory of Fred flashed thru my mind. He had referred to our company as "our baby."

"Our baby has cancer," he cried. "LuAn, if we have to travel the world over, let's find a cure for that cancer—and it will get well—it will live and thrive. Honey, please help me!" In that second, I realized he had taken it one step further and searched the heavens. Together we had done it! Now I knew . . . my decision was heaven sent! "Helen, you go, girl!" That's when I realized it was time for the mother bird to push the baby from the nest and let it soar on the wings of an angel!

As the largest major shareholder, I couldn't provide Mitchell's with the funding it needed to move to the next level and seize bigger opportunities. I had done the alliance. Now, an individual shareholder like me was more of a hindrance than an advantage. The company needed the right players—the cure. After Fred's death, I was the right player to lead our team. But as the company became more stable and needed to grow again, that was no longer the case. After careful evaluation and soul searching, I realized it was time to move on. But first, I had to get the okay from my family, who was speechless watching wacky mommy and now truly a blushing bride. I looked at my beautiful family with new eyes just like with Fred in those final moments. But that was then and this is now. I had to stay in the present moment, not regress, and I had to re-instill the idea that I was sane to my family members; it might not be easy.

I called a family meeting and told my husband and children about my thought, and what was bubbling up inside of me. "A part of me doesn't want to leave," I admitted, "a part of my heart will always be there, but my instincts tell me it's time." My family agreed and saw the logic; they even saw the genius. I put in the call to Schneiders, who were only too happy to purchase my shares in the company, I am proud to announce. They recognize the value of the Mitchell's name and have left our operation intact, operating under our family name, and continuing with our hard work, our good people, and our proud tradition.

U of S Gets $1 Million Donation

I strongly believe in the importance of giving back. Whether it's your time or your money, we all have the ability to support the causes that are important to us. Our local university was very important in my family's life. My father, the schoolteacher, graduated from the University of Saskatchewan and returned there many times to take upgrading courses. I credit my father with my love of learning, and I wanted to create a legacy in my parents' name. It was a proud day when my family and I announced the Gingara Trust Fund, a $1 million fund named in honor of my parents. And maybe even the mythical character, Gingara, too! Why not! Buddha's ladder of success made of jewels—just like the legend! This donation will help countless individuals—that's my thought!

I credit the University of Saskatchewan with building not just its community, province, country, and world—really—but contributing to a better world. It was at that university, in 1951, that a major breakthrough in cancer treatment was made with the colbalt-60 cancer therapy unit. Also known as the "cobalt bomb," the university is credited with revolutionizing treatment of cancer located deep in the body. It is estimated that the discovery has helped more than 7 million people around the world.

Not too dissimilar to our open "corporate cancer," the human form, got a boost here in my hometown, too! More recently, the University of Saskatchewan made headlines around the world when one of its research teams uncovered evidence that the traditional model of the human menstrual cycle is wrong. This modern-day discovery by university researchers will lead to the design of new, safer, and more effective contraception as well as improve reproductive technology for women who are having trouble conceiving. I am sure this will revolutionize healings for women and families everywhere!

I also recently made a large dona-
tion to the Cystic Fibrosis Foundation.

Cystic fibrosis changed my life;
now I hope to change the lives of
people with this awful disease. I knew
nothing about CF when Fred was diag-
nosed with the disease just prior to
our marriage. Since then, I've learned
enough to fill a textbook. But the most

> *Whether it's your time or your money, we all have the ability to support the causes that are important to us.*

important thing for me is that two of my children carry the CF gene
which, by the way, is related to chromosome number seven: Fred's
favorite number! As Fred's offspring, Freddie, Jr. and Jinji carry the
gene. Although they do not have the disease, they risk having children with CF if their spouses carry the gene. Fortunately, testing can
reduce this risk and our family will be done with the tragedy of CF.
But there are so many families who are coping with this terrible afflic-
tion. If I can help even one person avoid the pain and suffering Fred
endured, I will enjoy a satisfaction beyond compare.

WHY DOES YOUR LIFE
HAVE TO BE AN OPEN BOOK?

Not long after my marriage to Reese, I became pregnant. Reese
and I were overjoyed. Although I had just turned 42 at the time, I
was in good shape and had experienced easy pregnancies with all three
children. We announced the pregnancy at a family meeting with our
children, and they were equally excited. Several weeks into the pregnancy, we had an ultrasound. We could see our beautiful baby and
see the strong heartbeat. But a couple of days later, I began to spot.
When the bleeding got heavy, the doctor ordered another ultrasound.
The heartbeat was gone: Our baby was dead.

Reese and I were so very sad and immediately began to look for answers. As we humans have a tendency to do, we blame ourselves—showing no mercy. A very athletic man who played hard, Reese thought he might have been too hard on his body when he was younger. I worried about the impact of being on birth control for many years. Our doctor stopped us saying, "We don't know why this happened. We know there's a power much bigger than us at work. For whatever reason, it was right for it to be like this." *How right he is,* I thought.

> *As we humans have a tendency to do, we blame ourselves—showing no mercy.*

On our melancholy drive home, Reese said, "You aren't going to put this in the book, are you?"

I told him that I probably would.

"Why does your life have to be an open book?" he angrily demanded. (I guess it is not just us girls who can get hormonal now and then.)

"Because I'm on a mission," I replied. "I've seen lives that have been helped and changed because I've been open and honest about the challenges I've faced—families who have bonded, people who have achieved things they didn't think were possible, people who have started to love and accept themselves for the first time. That's why my life is an open book." I reminded my dear Reese that it has always been this way for me. My life has been exposed to the public for a long time, and I was on this journey when he met me. The difference was that now he was involved, and his number had come up.

He thought for a few moments and then said, as he placed his loving hand on my shoulder stroking my hair: "Actually, I love you even more because you're doing this."

And I felt blessed once again to be with a strong man who accepts me the way I am. We were both shaken, but not stirred.

SHOULD I SET THIS GUY FREE?

Strangely, this miscarriage brought back many of the feelings I had when I was 16 and pregnant. Back then, I felt ashamed that I had failed my parents. Now, 26 years later, I was grumpy, lumpy, and hormonal. I had failed my husband. I was depressed and agonizing over risking my health and sanity with another pregnancy. Reese would possibly never have the experience of having a biological child with me and never go through the precious moments like rocking our baby to sleep at night, watching the first steps, listening to the first words, saying it looks like you, or giggling about moments with a woman like me.

In my depressed and very fragile state with our dead child still inside my body, I saw only one scary option in the darkest of dark moments: I began to think fast thoughts. *Should I set this guy free?* I thought. Then I caught myself and I wondered if Fred ever thought that about me, the young wife nursing her ill husband, the one who was told he would never father a child. But I never considered leaving Fred even before our miracles began to happen. How could I think Reese would be different from me?

As it turns out, my children had similar thoughts. At a family meeting shortly after the miscarriage, they voiced a concern that maybe I was too old to have another baby. (Ouch. That one hurt!) When the children hinted of their concern that he would think of leaving me for a younger woman with whom he could have children, Reese took huge offense. Later, he took the children aside and assured them with words and Daddy bear hugs, splashed with kisses galore that he would never leave me. "I took my marriage vows very seriously," he told them. "This is my family, and you are our children."

Saved by an Attitude of Gratitude

Like any experience, there was a seed for good in this loss. Our family became closer. Reese and I realized our family couldn't be more complete. That night, when Reese and I were tucking Jinji into bed, she threw her arms around us and said, "I would have such a big hole in my heart if I didn't have you as my mom and Daddy as my daddy. I love him with my whole heart." Her simple expression of love took my breath away. *How easily we take all the gifts in the world for granted,* I thought later that night.

> *It's impossible to feel sorry for yourself or angry if you're giving thanks.*

Immediately, I demanded of myself to refocus and give thanks because it's impossible to feel sorry for yourself or angry if you're giving thanks. Try it. Giving thanks sparks something in you, and it's a wonderful healing energy. I wonder: Have you hugged and been hugged lately? A real bear hug—a bear-it-all kind of hug! Try it; that's the power.

LuAn Mitchell-Halter: You Ought to Be in Pictures!

A life in the headlines can take you many places—even to the movies. My life story has caught the attention of movie executives and may even come to the big screen. I got a kick out of how a British reporter described me:

"If you can envision Michelle Pfeiffer as a meat packer—say 'pork'—then you're onto her. Throw in the fighting spirit of Erin Brockovich and the business savvy of Martha Stewart and you're getting close to the real deal. Add the personal tragedy of a Kennedy wife and a dash of Mother Teresa and you'll be well on your way to envisioning LuAn Mitchell."

Now I'm sure the nuns at my high school weren't comparing me to Mother Teresa when I dropped the bombshell that I was pregnant in Grade 12. And while my husband might be smart enough to agree with the Michelle Pfeiffer comparison, my kids keep me grounded enough to know that I'm neither Erin nor Martha—I'm "Mom!" The important thing is not to start believing your own press clippings. While some articles can be complimentary, others will take potshots like the recent write-up in a national newspaper that said, "LuAn has portrayed herself as an entrepreneur." This was published after I had been named Canada's #1 Female Entrepreneur for the third year running. It wasn't just me calling myself an entrepreneur!

Sometimes, the media likes to build people up—then tear them down. I can't control what's said in the media, so I just go about my business, sharing my inspirational message and seizing every possible opportunity to plant a seed for good. If the media or moviemakers like my story, that's great. But if they all disappeared tomorrow, I would keep moving forward, following my three steps: make a realistic plan that will get you closer to your dream, follow your God-given instincts, and find the seed for good.

It's Full Steam Ahead
for LuAn Mitchell

Just as my pregnancy transported me back to my teenage years, my speaking career has also brought me full circle. For so many years, I was the girl in the audience who came from nowhere and knew nothing. But I was a sponge, soaking up the all the wonderful information I could find. Then I started using this advice in my daily life. I'm convinced I couldn't have survived the challenges life has thrown at me without the teaching of my many mentors—that includes my husband and children. It seems every moment has so many blessings and opportunities. And now, I've become a headliner—I've become a mentor, taking my message and helping others.

Recently, I joined a Women's Empowerment Team and found myself on the same speaking roster as one of my first mentors. I share the same publishing company as many of the authors I've read and admired. I am represented by a speaker's agency that also acts for some of my magnificent teachers. I sit at head tables with political leaders and respected business gurus. It has happened: I find myself on the same stage as these people I've admired for so long. Finally, I have the opportunity to answer my calling—to openly speak, to share, and to teach.

At the same time, I'm still learning. My journey is far from being finished. I still read, listen to tapes and CDs, visit Websites and watch videos daily. My teachers continue to grow in number. When I exercise, I work out my mind, body, and spirit. Usually, I listen to an audiotape that provides me with powerful ideas, read on my treadmill, do mental exercises, and good self-talk to myself so that I may in turn give out excellent advice. These teachers in our world—everywhere—help to keep me on the right path.

I couldn't have survived the challenges life has thrown at me without the teaching of my many mentors.

Every morning, I wake up and give thanks for the wonderful people in my life. My adventures with Mitchell's has made me one of the most appreciative and blessed people because of the fine people who surrounded me there, who accepted me, and who helped and were committed to attaining dreams side-by-side. So yes, my life is an open book. I have no taboos, no secrets, nothing to hide. After all, it's been a life lived in the headlines.

But remember where I came from—a small farming town in Northern Canada. And remember my start in life—a teenage pregnancy.

At first glance, it might seem that my marriage to Fred Mitchell assured me a life on easy street. Sure, if caring for a chronically ill man, living in a broken down van, and becoming a widow at the age of 37 is your definition of easy street! But despite what life threw at me, I never gave up. I kept getting up

> *Keep moving doggedly in the direction of your dream. It can come true. It will come true*

off the mat, dusting myself off, and continuing the fight. My point is that it worked for me, and it can work for you. Soak up information and ideas. Then make them yours. Start making changes in how you live and how you think. Don't cut yourself down, and never let fear get in your way. Don't shy away from risk. Trust your instincts. Keep moving doggedly in the direction of your dream. It can come true. It *will* come true—maybe even bigger and better than you ever thought possible!

Find your passion in life. And never ever give up on your dreams.

MY PLAN TO GET ME CLOSER TO MY DREAM:

Make the leap from student to teacher. Help others by putting my story "out there."

MY INSTINCTS:

I can help others by telling my story.

THE SEED FOR GOOD:

My story is a powerful force for good.

Reading Group Guide

ear Readers,

I'm delighted that you have chosen *Paper Doll* to bring into a group for discussion. It is my fondest wish that this book will motivate you to learn more about your dreams and will further support you in beginning to realize them. I trust that you will find the insights in this book useful in achieving a more satisfying life.

To help you in this quest, I offer below a study guide with questions to start you thinking and launch the conversations. It is up to you how you handle these thoughts and questions. You may use this at a onetime gathering, or better yet, allow your group to come together over a number of sessions. The guide I have created is rooted in the *Life Lessons* and *The Three Steps* written about in the book.

Now's the time. . . . Let go . . . Just imagine the freedom—believe . . . it's time to uncover yourself.

As you move forward, *know* that you are not alone.

I am with you on your journey, as are the many who came before us refusing to live their lives as "paper dolls."

In the words of a woman who was surely no one's *paper doll*, Amelia Earhart:

> The most difficult thing is the decision to act,
> the rest is merely tenacity.
> The fears are paper tigers.
> You can do anything you decide to do.
> You can act to change and control your life;
> and the procedure, the process is its own reward.

You're the "dressing" this world's been waiting for . . .

Dream Big!

— LuAn

1: Who we are goes well beneath the outer appearance of what we choose to wear. We have all had a situation in our lives where we have allowed others to underestimate us, or where we were misjudged. When was that for you, and how did it make you feel? What did you do to dispel that judgment?

2: I have tried to present you with some of the lessons I have learned along my journey. What was the most important Life Lesson for you in the book? Why did you relate to that particular lesson?

3: The more often we are able to give definition to our dream, the clearer it becomes. The clearer it becomes, the better our connection to the positive universal forces that can support our dream toward becoming a reality. How clearly is your dream defined? Can you describe it for the group?

4: No matter what your goal, you probably can't get there on your own. One of the best lessons I learned was to pay attention to those I admired and to surround myself with excellent people for support. Look to the people who have the traits, qualities, and behaviors that you desire to emulate. Share with the group who inspires you, who you admire, and who you see comes closest to doing what you dream of doing. Why did you choose them?

5: As we move closer to our dream, quite often, our priorities need to be revisited to assess whether they are still appropriate to where we are now in the course of our journey. Sometimes, that assessment must happen "in the moment" as it has quite often in my life. Are the priorities you set in the beginning still valid and suitable for your "plan" now? Are you willing to adjust your priorities as needed? What would dictate a change in your priorities?

6: Each of us has a voice inside that can help us when making difficult decisions. When we take time to listen and follow that voice, we will discover one of our greatest advocates for success in whatever we do—our instinctive, intuitive voice. It takes time to be in the stillness to learn which voice is the "true voice" and which is not. Usually we end up second-guessing our inner guidance, only to walk full on into crisis or disharmony. Share with the group a time when you clearly followed the true inner voice, and tell what happened. Now share a time when you did not. How did it differ?

7: There have been times when I clearly could have allowed the fear of the unknown to stop me in my tracks. Those are the times when I have relied heavily on my faith and hope. Hope keeps my faith fueled no matter what challenge I come up against. If you believe strongly in your dream, and it carries a "seed for good," then nothing can stop you. What challenges do you perceive you might meet on the path toward your dream? Do you believe you deserve to have your dream manifested? Then what are the real concerns?

8: There will be those days when you are ambushed by something out of the blue, and you want to give up. Those days are clearly the days you must get up and move on. And there will be days when something someone says will bring you to your knees. It is on those days when you focus on taking the high road and maintaining what's important. Those days are when it is important to have your "touchstones" to lean on. Share with the group a time when you were ambushed and made it through anyway. What got you through?

THE SEED FOR GOOD:

When we have a dream that is truly coming from the core of who we are, connected to our own personal "gift," we came to share with the world, it will burn inside us until it is realized. How will achieving your dream support you and the planet?

About LuAn

*A*s *an entrepreneur*, corporate executive, author, motivational speaker, philanthropist, and mother, LuAn Mitchell-Halter has lived a life of wide experience, harsh reality, and repeated triumph.

Mitchell-Halter has reached the pinnacle of business success being named Canada's Number One Female Entrepreneur for three successive years by *Chatelaine* and *Profit* magazines. On the international stage, she has been honored annually since 2001 by the Leading Women Entrepreneurs of the World. McGill University of Montreal has named LuAn as the 2003 recipient of the McGill Management Achievement Award for excellence of achievement in business and community service.

LuAn's business experience began with her own salon, spa, and modeling school, and included—as Chair of the Board of Directors— shepherding Mitchell's Gourmet Foods from the brink of bankruptcy to one of Canada's most successful value-added food processors. Her life is a story of struggle and survival. From the country kid who was taunted as "Elly Mae" at her high school, to the confident mother of three young children who rose to command one of Canada's largest food processing companies, she has always triumphed although she has also endured much.

She grew up in Saskatchewan, Canada, representing the City of Saskatoon in 1984 in the Miss Canada Pageant.

Children's literacy and environmental awareness are among LuAn's many interests. She has written several children's stories and visited many schools to give readings. From 1990 to 1994, she served as an advisor to "Kids for Saving Earth, North America." She also holds a patent on "Save the Planet," an environmental board game she invented.

Mitchell-Halter is an active community volunteer, having served on the Board of Directors of several charitable organizations, including the United Way, YWCA, and Junior Achievement.

Mitchell-Halter is President and CEO of Save The Planet Holdings, and led Mitchell's Gourmet Foods from 1998 to 2003 as Chair of the Board. She serves on several outside boards including The Leading Women Entrepreneurs of the World, Harvard University's John F. Kennedy School of Government Women's Leadership Board, and the University of Saskatchewan's Institute of Agricultural, Rural, and Environmental Health. LuAn is in constant demand as a motivational speaker, and she has appeared on the internationally acclaimed *Hour of Power* television broadcast as featured guest of Rev. Robert Schuller.

LuAn Mitchell-Halter believes a unified, happy family is life's greatest achievement. She recently remarried and lives with her husband, Dr. Reese Halter, and their three children in the family's dream home in Banff, Alberta, Canada.